CHEESE CHAMPIONS

THE WORLD'S CRÈME DE LA CRÈME
OF RAW MILK CHEESE

Lannoo

CONTENTS

9	**WHY 'REAL CHEESE' IS TIMELY AND IMPORTANT**
11	**INTRODUCTION**
19	**KARDITSEL** sensible, yet stubborn
30	*taste profile Aurélie*
33	**CHEESE AFFINEURS VAN TRICHT** cheese aged to perfection
44	*taste profile Herve pikant*
46	*taste profile Cabriolait*
49	**REMEKER** working with nature
60	*taste profile Remeker*
63	**WRÅNGEBÄCK** remaking the oldest cheese brand in Sweden
74	*taste profile Wrångebäck Ost*
77	**CRAVERO** Parmigiano Reggiano with a heritage
88	*taste profile Parmigiano reggiano*

91	**FORMAGGI DEBBENE** organic Pecorino from Sardinia
100	*taste profile Pecorino*
103	**L'ETIVAZ AOP** an artisan product from an alpine lifestyle
114	*taste profile L'Etivaz AOP*
117	**NEAL'S YARD DAIRY** selecting and maturing outstanding British cheese
128	*taste profile Montgomery*
130	*taste profile Baron Bigod*
133	**STICHELTON** the real King of English cheese
142	*taste profile Stichelton*
145	**BWLCHWERNEN FAWR** the longest standing registered organic dairy farm in Wales
154	*taste profile Hafod Welsh Cheddar*

157 APPLEBY'S DAIRY
award-winning Cheshire since 1952

168 taste profile Appleby's cheshire

171 FROMAGERIE DONGÉ
authentic and artisanal Brie de Meaux

180 taste profile Brie de Meaux

183 JOSEPH PACCARD
artisanal maturation of raw milk Reblochon

194 taste profile Reblochon
196 taste profile Beaufort Haut Alpage AOP

199 MAISON MONS
in search of the best traditional cheeses

206 taste profile Salers Tradition

209 JASPER HILL FARM
hand-crafted European-style cheeses made in the US

220 taste profile Bayley Hazen Blue

224   **MORE TASTE MAKERS**

230   *taste profile Comté AOP*

232   *taste profile Mont d'Or AOP*

234   *taste profile Roquefort Le Vieux Berger*

236   *taste profile Langres AOP*

238   *taste profile Zamorano AOP*

240   *taste profile Picón Bejes-Tresviso AOP*

242   *taste profile Humo*

247   **ACKNOWLEDGEMENTS**

248   **COLOFON**

Why 'real cheese' is timely and important

As the implications of intensive farming and industrial-scale food production make themselves felt across the globe, there has never been more focus on how our food is produced, how it tastes, and how good (or not) it is for us and the planet. Against this backdrop, the publication of the first collection that introduces the raw milk farm-made cheeses from around the world and the people behind them – be they maker, monger or affineur – feels particularly well timed.

In *Cheese Champions: The world's crème de la crème of raw milk cheese,* we finally have a book that comprehensively explains the work that goes into these cheeses. We can see the kind of food systems we as consumers support through buying them, and how and why spending more money on real cheese than one might on its mass-produced equivalent can deliver better value in terms of flavour, nutrition, and ethical and environmental responsibility. After working at Neal's Yard Dairy for some 30 years, for the past 10 as a director, I have had the privilege of meeting many of the people and eating many of the cheeses featured in this book – but it is increasingly important that they and their intrinsic qualities reach a larger audience.

Neal's Yard Dairy's activities as a monger, maturer and exporter of cheese have allowed us the opportunity over the years to engage with similar businesses facing similar challenges in many countries. In the face of those challenges, the community of people who work with real cheese is becoming increasingly dynamic and integrated. It is to this network that our book pays tribute. And it is by extending this network even wider, bringing into its reach those who eat the cheese as well as those who make it, that it will continue to strengthen and endure.

Jason Hinds,
Sales Director Neal's Yard Dairy Londen

Introduction

WHY PUBLISH A BOOK ABOUT "REAL CHEESE"?

In early 2018, we met up over a pint and a good meal. By we, I mean Frederic Van Tricht from Kaasaffineurs van Tricht and Giedo De Snijder from Kaasmakerij Karditsel. The meeting in itself wasn't particularly special because we made an effort to get together once every few months. What was unique was the invariably candid conversations between a cheese affineur and a cheese producer about the ins and outs of our cheese business, our collaboration, and how the cheese market we were involved in was evolving. Those meetings were enriching and invaluable.

As a result of our shared passion and experiences with raw milk cheese, in the summer of 2018 we had the idea of putting together a cheese book in which the champions of the international cheese scene would talk about how they produce and ripen authentic cheese – cheese that irrefutably makes a difference, both in terms of taste and intrinsic value.

We were undoubtedly inspired to so by the book *Reinventing the Wheel: Milk, microbes and the fight for real cheese* by Bronwen and Francis Percival, which was published in 2017. In this book, the authors first discuss what was lost when industrial cheese replaced artisanal cheese, which is very much a product of the unique location where it's made. They then illustrated the changing landscape in the cheese world and how more artisanal cheesemakers and affineurs are discovering the special bond between microbes, milk, and flavour. It is these stories about real cheese that we want to bring extensively to light in this book.

WHAT IS REAL CHEESE?

Cheese always tells a story. It says something about the location, the dairy animals, and the people that make it. It originates from the soil and grows from a longing to create something beautiful and nutritious. It's been that way for centuries, but does that still apply today?

In little over a century, industrial preparation methods have altered every aspect of the cheesemaking process, from the animals that produce the milk to the microbial strains that ferment the cheese, to the production methods used.

Raw milk has gradually been marginalized under the pretence that it is a threat to public health – following an intensive lobbying effort by the economically powerful food industry, which profited most from pasteurizing milk to supply the same standardized product time and time again.

Over many generations, that industrialization has led to a monumental shift in preferences and tastes. Consumers no longer wanted tantalizing, creamy, or sharp, pungent cheeses; mild-flavoured cheeses, price, and shelf life had become the main buying incentives.

In response to this anonymous uniformity underpinning the apparent abundance of cheeses in cheese displays, a countermovement arose from a renewed way of thinking that focused on the biodiversity of the pasture, the dairy animals, and the microflora of the dairy farm. This

is a promising development that shows us in practical terms why the more distinctive and flavourful cheeses deserve a place at our tables. Moreover, this approach has led to a revival of artisanal cheese production, partly thanks to modern consumers' demand for quality foods that are locally and traditionally produced.

Compared to the overwhelming industrialization of cheese, traditional preparation methods not only lead to better quality and an authentic character but also to increased food safety and sustainability. That is why we not only want to talk about making cheese but also about farming the milk for the cheese; just like fine wine, good cheese is largely determined by the quality of its ingredients. Farm and flavour are inextricably linked. Cheese is unique in that respect because, with the right production methods, cheese can bring together the biodiversity of three different worlds: flora, fauna and microbiota – in a way that is reflected in the flavour cheese enthusiasts taste. In other words, real cheese allows us to taste an entire agricultural system. It's a model for how ecological and sustainable food production should look and be experienced in the future.

WHAT ARE REAL CHEESEMAKERS?

The time is ripe for a book that puts the crème de la crème of the contemporary international cheese scene on the map – a book written by a group of exemplary cheesemakers from Europe and America who devote their passion, expertise and experience to offering cheese with intrinsic quality to the consumer every single day. The result is a series of portraits of people and cheeses illustrating what makes real cheese special and what unique flavours they create. It's the best way to show what it takes to produce and conserve authentic cheese.

We hope that this book provides an inspirational journey through our globally shared cultural history and gives insight into the tensions at play between progress, modernity, and tradition. This book aims to provide a clear, comprehensible tour of the fascinating world of traditional cheese production through text and images. That is why this book will be published in two editions: a Dutch and an English version.

Each story touches on the following themes:
- *the cheese culture in the various countries;*
- *the personal cheese journey of the cheesemaker or affineur;*
- *how their passion for and vision of real cheese grew;*
- *the incentives, guiding principles, expectations and challenges that they face in their day-to-day operations;*
- *a few final words for the cheese world;*
- *a featured cheese with a taste profile and pairing tips.*

Sadly, we do not have enough room to highlight all of the real cheesemakers and affineurs in this book. That is why we have selected 15 trendsetters from Europe and North America, thereby trying to bring as many different cheese varieties as possible to light. In the acknowledgements, we have included a list of producers that we haven't been able to do justice to in this book but who certainly deserve to be mentioned. Who knows, perhaps we'll follow up with a second book with trendsetters if this book manages to inspire the international cheese world and leaves it wanting more.

WHAT DOES REAL CHEESE TASTE LIKE?

Although wine and cheese are very similar when it comes to assessing their intrinsic value, there are still no standards for the appraisal of cheeses like those we have for wines. Still, like wine, cheese can easily be assessed on characteristics such as texture, aromas and flavours, albeit with slightly modified criteria. We can similarly discern primary, secondary, and tertiary aromas and describe the mouthfeel.

Analysing how and why a cheese develops certain aromas, flavours, and textures provides us with valuable insight into its primary ingredient (milk), the production process and the maturation process. The question then arises: why aren't there any grand-cru cheeses like there are grand-cru wines?

Jasper Hill Farm, an American cheese dairy in Vermont – which you can read about in a later chapter of this book – has developed a model for their customers describing the sensory qualities of their cheeses. The dairy farm uses the model to clearly communicate the characteristics of the different cheese batches and their corresponding profiles. Jasper Hill was so kind as to provide us with their concept of the sensory model for this book.

The taste profile that you will find at the end of each chapter is based on Jasper Hill's model in a slightly modified and simplified form. But, make no mistake: behind this simplified form lies an extensive taste test with professional tasting and evaluation by one and the same person. Professional wine taster, Charlotte Nauwelaerts, took on this important task with dedication and verve. Charlotte has a Level 4 diploma from the internationally renowned WSET (Wine & Spirit Education Trust), whose programme participants are prepared for the most prestigious jobs in the wine industry through intensive theoretical and practical training. She also uses this extensive experience in cheese tasting to recognize and define their various aromas. For ten years, Charlotte has worked at Elsen Kaasambacht in Leuven (Belgium), one of the most famous cheesemongers in the Benelux. Her daily work consists of ripening and tasting cheese. You will find Charlotte on Instagram at @charlotte_and_wine.

We have included an example to illustrate which basic characteristics form the basis of the taste profiles you will find in this book. L'Etivaz AOP is a hard, Swiss, raw milk cheese, produced during the summer months from May to October in the alpine pastures of the Vaud Alps. The cheese has a firm texture, and its dominant aromas are roasted and herbal. After this brief summary follows a more extensive description of the flavours.

	CHARACTERISTIC	VALUE
TEXTURE	*Firmness*	*8.5*
AROMA	*Animal*	*6*
AROMA	*Herbal*	*7*
AROMA	*Roasted*	*7*
AROMA	*Fruity*	*4*
AROMA	*Vegetal*	*0*
AROMA	*Lactic*	*0*
AROMA	*Mineral*	*0*
FLAVOUR	*Sweet*	*3*
FLAVOUR	*Salty*	*6*
FLAVOUR	*Acidic*	*0*
FLAVOUR	*Bitter*	*0*
FLAVOUR	*Umami*	*4*

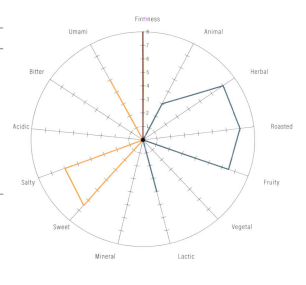

WHAT IS OUR MISSION?

We want to raise awareness in a world where many people have become indifferent to intrinsic quality and authentic flavour. With this book, we invite people to take notice, respect and become involved with the bigger story that links everything together, a story that we believe truly matters.

We hope that the testimonials in this book will offer insight to cheese professionals, chefs, cheese enthusiasts and foodies alike. We hope that these stories inspire everyone who loves cheese but has never considered its value, meaning, or potential. But above all, we hope that this book leaves you hungry for a piece of delicious, authentic cheese.

Giedo De Snijder and Frederic Van Tricht, September 2021

KARDITSEL
sensible yet stubborn

CHEESEMAKER

GIEDO DE SNIJDER
Kaasmakerij Karditsel
Founded in 2015
Lummen, Limburg
BELGIUM

WWW.KARDITSEL.BE

SINCE 2000, GOAT'S CHEESE HAS BECOME SUCH A SUCCESS THAT VARIOUS SMALLER PRODUCERS ARE BEING SWALLOWED WHOLE BY THE MARKET'S LARGE INDUSTRIAL PLAYERS.

HOME-GROWN CHEESE CULTURE

Belgium has historically never touted itself as a cheese-producing country, although it has always marketed itself as a country rich in milk, butter, and cream. But even if we do not have a traditional cheesemaking culture, we do have two renowned cheeses: Brussels cheese and Herve cheese. The "real" Brussels cheese has been considered dead and buried since 2018. Herve is apparently the only Belgian cheese that can hold its own well enough to have earned a European Protected Designation of Origin status.

Brussels cheese, also known as *hettekees* (smelly cheese) originated in the Zenne region southwest of Brussels, home of the renowned Lambic and gueuze beers. The history of Brussels cheese dates back as far as the fifteenth century and perhaps even further. Soft cheese, also known as "cloetcaes" according to a plaque dating from 1683, was the most common type of cheese found on Brabant farmsteads. The Brussels cheese was a direct descendant of this type of cheese.

In the twentieth century, this cheese found its home in the Brussels region, where it became known far and wide as food for the "common working man". There are two reasons why Brussels cheese lost its status as a low-fat cheese. On the one hand, strict European regulations made the traditional drying and ripening process impossible. On the other hand, the high salt content no longer fitted in with changing consumption patterns. With its pungent smell and tangy flavour, Brussels cheese was not a cheese for the faint-hearted.

By contrast, Herve cheese from the Walloon region, which originated around 1250 in the Duchy of Limburg, fits well into the northern French cheese tradition of washed-rind cheeses. Later, Herve cheese also became known as Remoudou and made its way to the New World, imported by immigrants, under the name Limburger cheese, the working-class cheese. The name Remoudou has a historical background. In the sixteenth century, Holy Roman Emperor Charles V ordered the farmers to convert their farmlands into meadows. During that time, the cheese was named Remoudou, from the French word *remoudre* (to milk again). The farmers paid the landowners according to the amount of milk they produced. As a result, they did not fully milk their cows and held back the richest milk for personal use.

Around 1900, cheese was a relatively scarce luxury product in Belgium. Commercial and industrial cheese production did not really take off until after 1940. Under orders from the German occupiers during the Second World War, Belgium started producing young, semi-hard and hard cheeses which were strongly influenced by Dutch cheeses such as Gouda. From the 1960s onwards, Cheddar- and Emmentaler-inspired cheeses entered the market, and from 1970 even Italian cheeses were introduced. In short, the Belgian cheese landscape showed extraordinarily little authenticity or innovation.

This finally started to change in 1980 with the introduction of Passendale and raw-milk Wijnendale cheeses from the Passendale cheese factory. In the eighties, the first small, artisanal cheesemakers started appearing, such as Het Hinkelspel in Flanders and Fromagerie du Gros Chêne in the Walloon region.

In Flanders, these cheesemakers were mostly a new generation seduced into the trade; newcomers who, having no cheesemaking history to draw from, brought innovative change to the cheese landscape with their out-of-the-box thinking.

Since 2000, goat's cheese has become such a success that various smaller producers are being swallowed whole by the market's large industrial players. To counterbalance this general scaling up of cheese production, a new wave of artisanal cheese factories started up in 2015, businesses that have everything it takes to give Belgian cheese a distinctive character once and for all. They started to meet the growing consumer demand for high-quality and locally produced cheeses.

OUT OF THE BOX

I spent my childhood in a village on the outskirts of an industrial region. Back then it was a relatively rural area; it is now squeezed in between ring roads and industrial estates. The village was literally and figuratively a place to spend the night for hundreds of factory workers who earned their daily bread around Vilvoorde and Brussels. I lived in one of the worker's houses and we were blessed with a baker, butcher, and a grocer on the other side of the street. Saturdays, as I recall, were special. That was when, unlike the rest of the week, we would have bread for dinner and I was allowed to choose my own sandwich filling at the grocers. My favourite: a firm wedge of brie, deliciously slimy under the white crust. With every bite of brie that melted on my tongue, half a slice of bread followed. I know that children are easy to please, but those Saturdays will always remain etched into my hard drive with the label "good mood food". It was only much later that I discovered the type of brie that was responsible for my childhood taste orgasm.

Was it written in the stars? Against all odds, I became a self-taught cheesemaker at some point. How did that happen? I was born a little too late to consciously experience the turbulent times in 1968 and ended up at university in 1972. The world as we had known it until then was facing huge challenges; it seemed to me that contributing to this change would be more effective than pretending to be a student. After a few years of left-wing palaver and meetings, I took stock of what little we had to show for it. I had had enough of spouting big ideas and wanted to move forward in a clear direction. I happened to come into contact with the back-to-the-land movement and the drive for self-sufficiency which had made its way to Belgium from the USA. I was instantly sold, moved to the countryside, and started growing my own vegetables, baking bread, making wine, keeping

goats, making cheese and so on. At night, I worked as a night watchman. In 1983, this way of life gave rise to the Midgard, a name with plenty of ecological symbolism. It was not a seed farm or an organic farming business, but a goat farm because I had fallen in love with those stubborn four-footed animals people call goats. Starting a goat farm as a non-farmer in those years was not exactly a matter of course. At the weekly markets where we tried to sell our cheese, people would pass by holding their noses and grimacing: "Ugh, goat's cheese… that stinks." In late 1986, we moved from our small, rented farm in Haacht to Werchter, where we built a cheese factory and a goat stall for 120 dairy goats from the ground up. This marked a new phase in our story that would last for the next 20 years. After two years of experimentation, we launched our very first semi-soft washed-rind goat's cheese (Roderic & C°) in early 1990. This was followed three years later by Merlijn, a Belgian ripened brie made from goat's cheese. They were the products of our active search for authentic cheeses with distinctive characteristics. Although highly praised by cheese connoisseurs and cheese enthusiasts, the market in the early nineties was not ready for our red-coloured gems. We lacked the critical mass and the means to adequately promote this unique product on the cheese market. However, it did teach us a lesson: people tend to stick to what they know. In 2006, our Werchter cheese adventure came to an abrupt halt due to an unsolvable wastewater issue. That led to the sudden sale of the Midgard cheese factory and thus ended our life as cheesemakers.

OUR CHEESE FACTORY LIVES ON BACTERIA, YEASTS, AND MOULDS. THROUGH CLIMATE CONTROL AND HYGIENE, WE ALLOW THE RIGHT BIOTOPES TO FLOURISH TO PROMOTE THE DEVELOPMENT OF DESIRABLE MICROFLORA AND DISCOURAGE THE GROWTH OF UNDESIRABLE FLORA.

Nonetheless, five years later I was once again bitten by the irresistible cheesemaking bug and we embarked on a passionate search for a viable way to pick up the cheese ladle once more. Convinced that the time was ripe for an inspiring, value-driven and full-flavoured cheese venture, I started a cheese factory in 2015 under a new name, Karditsel. That year I turned 60, and although some claimed that I was a little too old for a fresh start, it made perfect sense to me. After all, there is a reason why we say in the cheese world: *age is not important unless you are a cheese*.

KARDITSEL, FROM SCRATCH

Kaasmakerij Karditsel started out as a partnership between two farmers and two cheesemakers. This initially had far-reaching consequences for the young farmers. After all, they had decided to cancel their active milk contract for what was, at the time, little more than a theoretical concept thought up by a couple of old men. The young goat farm had imposed a ceiling with a maximum of 300 goats so that they could accommodate and care for them under the best possible conditions. It was a conscious move towards small-scale farming, far from the "goat factories" which house thousands of goats. What particularly drew us was the conscious preservation of a mix of common and increasingly rare domestic goat breeds. The business was organically certified and had all the potential to become even more sustainable in the long term. In short, the farm was the ideal location for producing raw-milk goat's cheese.
We weren't making this decision lightly. But how could we, as small-scale newcomers, distinguish ourselves in an already saturated cheese market? Doing the same thing everyone else was doing or doing it more cheaply was not an option for us. We needed to thoroughly analyse the cheese market and find our niche.
Although the market for goat's cheese had been growing rapidly since early 2000, local cheese suppliers sadly looked on as businesses were snatched up by large (often foreign) producers. The situation led to a limited and often industrially produced range of cheeses with little or no added value, let alone innovation. This was in stark contrast to the unmet demand from an increasingly large group of consumers, fed up with anonymous, uniform and bland food products who were looking for healthy, locally produced, authentic and flavourful foods to identify with.

We were convinced that the demand was out there, now all that was needed was the supply... which came about in a purely theoretical form. In 2012, I was given the opportunity to become cellar master at a renowned Belgian cheese shop, Elsen Kaasambacht in Leuven. The entire gamut of cheeses, including goat's cheeses, from all over the EU passed through my hands every week. After being away from the cheese market for over five years, any new market insights were more than welcome. This experience taught me a lot and ultimately also determined our selection of cheeses when Karditsel started up its production. After a month of tweaking, the plan was practically complete: we would produce a series of innovative semi-soft and soft goat's cheeses naturally smear-ripened. This range clearly stood out from the fresh and semi-hard cheeses offered by our competitors in the Low Countries. With expertise, experience and a sophisticated infrastructure and climate control, we would create our niche.

At Karditsel, two types of cheeses are made, mostly *pâte lactique* cheeses but also *pâte molle* cheeses. Those French cheese terms require an explanation. If you draw a scale on paper and on the left side include the fresh, soft dairy products (*pâte lactique*) and on the right side the hard dairy products (*pâte dure*), then you will find the *pâte molle* cheeses in the middle of that scale. *Pâte lactique* cheeses are cheeses primarily made through the conversion of milk sugars into lactic acid by lactic acid bacteria and a little rennet. The milk takes almost 24 hours to curdle before the cheese has enough mass and is solid enough for processing. On the other end of the scale are the hard cheeses, which produce the necessary cheese curds primarily through the action of the rennet. The curds are often ready to be processed after a mere 30 minutes. In the middle of the scale are the *pâte molle* cheeses which are created both through lactic acid production and the curdling action of the rennet. These are the hardest cheeses to make in terms of technique. Goat's cheeses are traditionally *pâte lactique* cheeses; the *pâte molle* cheeses include cheeses such as camembert, brie, munster, reblochon. At Karditsel, both cheese curd types are prepared using traditional techniques, hand-scooped with a ladle or a large-slotted spoon and dry-salted by hand later in the process. When handled with care and with respect for the fragile goat dairy product, the result is a cheese with an exceptionally fine texture. Our mixture of different goat breeds provides a distinctive milk flavour that, together with the natural flora and ripening agents in our milk, create the rich aromas that characterize our refined cheeses. This characteristic taste has led to plenty of national and international recognition over the past five years.

In the *pâte lactique* range, our absolute winners are Florence (type: Belgian brie), Aurélie (type: Sainte-Maure de Touraine with a Geotrichum rind) and Kato (type: Cathare). Our signature cheeses in the *pâte molle* range are Corneel (type: reblochon) and Paulette (type: péraïl). But the icing on the Karditsel cake, which I had been nurturing in my mind over the years, posed a greater challenge. Let's say we could innovate the cheesemaking process for one specific type of cheese by using purely plant-based rennet instead of animal-based or microbial rennet – namely rennet from the active components of the cardoon (*Cynara cardunculus*), a thistle related to the artichoke. The plant is an ethically responsible and sustainable alternative, a local innovation based on an ancient Southern European tradition. In April 2015, we won the agricultural Innovation Award from the Province of Limburg with this project, and in September 2015, we succeeded in launching and marketing our Corneel, a semi-soft washed-rind cheese. In contrast to traditional cardoon-based goat's cheeses, this Corneel was not bitter and provided a stable dairy product. In June 2018, the Corneel was awarded the bronze medal in the "soft washed-rind cheeses" category during the first Farm Cheese Awards in Lyon (France), an international cheese competition exclusively for farm-based, raw-milk cheese producers who do not use genetically manipulated organisms.

Our cheese factory lives on bacteria, yeasts, and moulds. Through climate control and hygiene, we allow the right biotopes to flourish to promote the development of desirable microflora and discourage the growth of undesirable flora. But we keep our hygiene in check. We constantly and conscientiously keep our cheese factory clean but not sterile. Our daily learning process involves trying to understand our microflora, not an easy task when you are processing raw milk in a farm environment under varying weather conditions.

Without an eye for detail, you will never stand out and always remain a mediocre player in a highly complex game. You need to be dedicated to craftsmanship. *Il faut être doué* (you have to be gifted), as the reblochon cheese farmers rightly say.

This would have been a time when many cheesemakers would have rested on their laurels, but not Karditsel; we have not reached our destination yet on our journey to the holy grail of artisanal cheese craftsmanship.

KARDITSEL, STANDING OUT FROM THE (GOAT) HERD

For the first five years, from 2015 until 2020, Karditsel was fully focused on the optimisation of production, commercialization and personnel. Unfortunately, the goat farm was unable to keep up with the growth of the cheese dairy due to disagreements between the two men who ran the farm. Only when those problems were solved, back in 2020, and one of the farmers took the reins firmly in hand, did the focus of the farm really lie on the symbiosis with Karditsel. It was finally time to stand out from the herd.

Farmers are the key to everything because they have an impact on the soil, the feed, the animals, how those animals are kept, the milking, and the storage of the milk. Then and only then does the processing of the milk into cheese begin.

The farm provides milk which is exceptionally suitable for cheese processing. In other words, dairy farming for cheesemaking comes before the cheese creating process. After all, what makes cheese unique is its capacity to combine the biodiversity of three different worlds – the flora, fauna and microbiota – into a form that can be tasted by the consumer.

Farms are natural sources of biodiversity which enables them to produce distinctive milk and, therefore, characteristic farm cheese that reflects the quality of this milk. "Authentic" cheese marries farming with flavour. The practice of embodying this flavour in cheese through centuries-old genetic microbial patrimony is, moreover, highly significant for our intestinal health. Researchers are convinced that modern-day diseases such as diabetes, asthma, obesity, auto-immune diseases, and atrophic pathological conditions are linked to the deterioration of our intestinal flora.

Strict European regulations have led to a re-evaluation of milk, now required to contain as few micro-organisms as possible. That is why we are now stuck with what might be considered "dead milk cheese" and an unprecedented monoculture in microbial terms. How can we once more create cheese from raw milk with a richer microbiological diversity and flavour potential? How do we incorporate farm-specific microbiological characteristics into our raw-milk cheese? That will be Karditsel's challenge from now on.

As a young farm and cheese factory, we cannot draw on the agricultural and financial foundations we would have had if there had been generations before us, nor can we draw on support from manufacturers' organisations and research institutions such as can be found in France, or

KARDITSEL

on financial support offered by government-funded or other agencies. But where there is a will, there is a way. With the help of French scientific resources, we have developed a plan of action to leverage and sustain a richer microbial diversity at farm level. This will constantly need to be monitored through biological analyses to enable us to measure the benefits and consciously weigh them up against the risks. That is a huge investment for a young, small-scale cheesemaker such as Karditsel.

We have been considering the idea of setting up a crowdfunding campaign for this project. If we can present the results of our project in a transparent fashion, it can help and motivate other artisanal cheesemakers in our region to take the next sustainable step to more microbial diversity and more authentic flavours.

FOOD THAT MAKES A DIFFERENCE

For almost 40 years, cheese has been a source of inspiration for me and the driving force behind a learning process into which I have poured my blood, sweat and tears. This determination to rise above the rest has also demanded a lot of sacrifices. Was it worth it? It has not made me rich in terms of money, but it has enriched me greatly by providing fertile ground for my stubborn nature. I hope that future generations will continue to strive to produce foods that make a difference and are a testament to the intrinsic values of sustaining man and nature. Perhaps the journey of a small Belgian cheesemaker such as Karditsel may serve as an inspiration.

IF WE CAN PRESENT THE RESULTS OF OUR PROJECT IN A TRANSPARENT FASHION, IT CAN HELP AND MOTIVATE OTHER ARTISANAL CHEESEMAKERS IN OUR REGION TO TAKE THE NEXT SUSTAINABLE STEP TO MORE MICROBIAL DIVERSITY AND MORE AUTHENTIC FLAVOURS.

KARDITSEL

TASTE PROFILE

AURÉLIE
Kaasmakerij Karditsel

Soft Belgian goat's cheese with a geotrichum rind

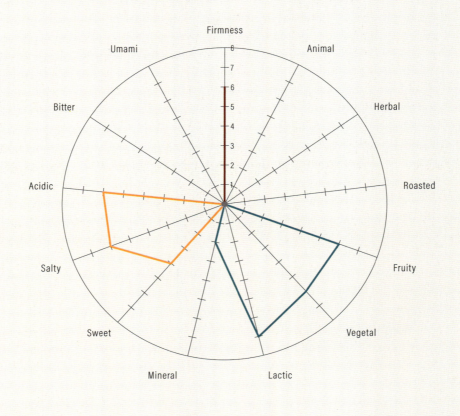

TEXTURE	**SOFT, STICKY AND CLAYEY**
DOMINANT FLAVOURS	**YOGURT**
	NUTS
	GRASS, HAY, STRAW
SUBTLE NOTES	**WET ROCKS**
	MOULD
	HEATHER
	BREAD DOUGH
WINE TIPS	**FRESH WHITE WINE, WHETHER OR NOT WITH GRASSY OR GREEN AROMAS**
	e.g. Sauvignon Blanc from a cool region

CHEESE AFFINEURS VAN TRICHT

cheese aged to perfection

CHEESE AFFINEUR

FREDERIC VAN TRICHT
Cheese affineurs Van Tricht
Founded in 1970
Antwerp, Antwerp
BELGIUM

WWW.KAASAFFINEURS-VANTRICHT.BE

THANKFULNESS IS CERTAINLY A RECURRING THEME IN MY CHEESE STORY. A STORY THAT WASN'T ENTIRELY PREDESTINED TO TURN OUT THE WAY IT DID BECAUSE I CERTAINLY WASN'T A CHEESE FAN BACK WHEN I WAS YOUNG.

FROM CHEF TO CHEESE AFFINEUR

The foundations of the Van Tricht cheese business were established in 1970 by my grandparents. My parents strengthened this foundation further and made the shop even more appealing, which led to new developments – such as our cheeses being added to restaurant menus. In 2015, my wife and I took over the reins and now it's up to us to write the next chapter in the family business. I am incredibly thankful to both my parents and our customers for having faith in us.

Thanks to them, we not only have a flourishing wholesale business but two fine shops. The wholesale side is located in the buildings of the De Koninck city brewery in Antwerp. Next to the brewing hall, where the Belgian beer "Het Bolleke" is still brewed, we allow our cheeses to mature in the former bottling plant. That's where we prepare our orders and send our cheeses to shops, restaurants and importers worldwide. Our flagship shop is Cheese Affineurs Van Tricht on the Fruithoflaan in the outskirts of Antwerp, which was recently taken over by my father's sister and Jo D'haene.

Finally, we also have Only Cheese by Cheese Affineurs Van Tricht, also located at the De Koninck brewery. This is where individuals can find our selection of perfectly aged cheeses. I call it our factory store: a smaller shop than the Fruithoflaan location and focused purely on cheese. Since we first set up shop in the brewery, we've acquired a number of flavourful neighbours, such as the excellent chocolatier, Jitsk. Then there's The Bakery, offering fresh, warm baked goods, and the best butcher in the country, De Laet-Van Haver/the Butcher's Store. There are also two restaurants: Black Smoke and The Butcher's Son, with one Michelin star.

In addition to my parents and customers, I am also thankful to all the passionate professionals and cheese enthusiasts I've met and learned to appreciate in my own country and far beyond. Thankfulness is certainly a recurring theme in my cheese story. A story that wasn't entirely predestined to turn out the way it did because I certainly wasn't a cheese fan back when I was young. I didn't start my cheese discovery journey until later in life. However, my love for delicious food was something I learned at my mother's knee, and that was the direction I wanted to take after completing my secondary education. In 1997, I started my culinary training at the hotel school in Koksijde, which continues to serve me well today when working with chefs. When I started looking for some extra work to complement my studies in 1999, it made perfect sense for me to help out in my parents' cheese shop. I started working at the wholesaler's, which was still located on the Fruithoflaan back then.

I soon found that I had been bitten by the same cheese bug that my father had. As an affineur, you are given the opportunity to work with the finest products and to make those excellent products even better. In 2001, after I graduated from the hotel school, I wanted to start work at the wholesaler's, but my father wouldn't let me on board just yet. My parents made me work in the shop for another year to learn the trade properly. I passed the test, and starting in 2003, my father and I were both representing Cheese Affineurs Van Tricht.

In 2015, my father retired, although he still helps whenever he can. Since then, I've been responsible for the daily operations on the wholesale side of the business. I arrange the selection, purchase and ripening of the cheeses; maintain customer contacts; prepare and deliver orders; attend fairs; and organise cheese tastings. I learnt most of my expertise on the job with my father, but I also like to learn from colleagues and cheesemakers. Working closely with others and exchanging ideas leads to an unbelievable synergy. Every time we import a local cheese from a small-scale farmer, it gives us this tremendous surge of energy. My training as a chef means that I'm always keeping my culinary customers in mind. I love to help search for the perfect cheese for every dish, and I like to experiment with cheeses myself. The dialogue with the customer and the cheesemaker always takes centre stage.

A LARGE INTERNATIONAL CHEESE FAMILY

It must have been 2005 when Jason Hinds walked into our lives to promote his Neal's Yard Dairy cheeses from the United Kingdom. Like many other cheese affineurs and cheesemakers, I consider him a bridge-builder in the cheese world with his many international contacts. He's a man who has not only brought his own vision but also those of many others to help shape the international cheese world. What makes Jason so unique is not only his extensive global network but particularly his gift for bringing all those people together in such an inspiring way. I had been interested in developing more contacts abroad for a while in order to export our Belgian cheeses, but this had largely remained a dream because

of our small-scale approach. It wasn't until we moved to the De Koninck brewery site in the summer of 2012 that we finally had a spacious new location which offered the right environment for trading Belgian cheese far beyond our national borders – as Neal's Yard Dairy has done for British cheeses.

Jason also put me in touch with one of the most prominent cheese figures in the United States: Adam Moskowitz. His father is one of the founders of the European quality cheese import trade in North America, and Adam himself is the man behind the Larkin Cold Storage and Columbia Cheese businesses in Long Island City in New York. He gained substantial fame in the cheese world with the Cheesemonger Invitational, which Adam set up in a storage facility on Long Island. One of the events during the invitational was an original competition for the best American cheesemonger. In 2012, I was invited to become a member of the jury. That was quite an honour, considering the event had a national reputation in the United States and is one of the leading events for generating interest for cheese selling as a trade. Today, similar events take place in San Francisco and Chicago.

I can rightly say that Adam Moskowitz has become my cheese link to the United States. But I have other excellent contacts in America, including Ihsan and Valerie Gurdal from Formaggio Kitchen. They own three shops in Boston and deliver cheese – including various Belgian varieties – to countless restaurants. Ihsan is widely known as a cheese sleuth who introduces many specialities from small-scale European producers across the pond to the American market.

My meetings with people like Jason Hinds, Adam Moskowitz and Ihsan Gurdal have inspired me tremendously and opened my eyes to new possibilities. They encouraged me to come out from behind the counter and visit international cheese events more often. Since then, I feel like I've become part of a large, international cheese family, something I'm incredibly proud of. Those contacts abroad are of great value to me. Talking with colleagues about what goes on in the artisan cheese world and which fabulous new cheeses are making their appearance only serves to increase my passion for cheese. And by that, I mean my passion for real cheese: raw milk cheese made using traditional methods, preferably at the farm.

This brings me to the typical, distinctive quality of raw milk cheese that I feel we can never stress enough. With industrially produced cheeses, the milk is pasteurised and skimmed because the fat content of milk varies depending on the season and the breed and type of cow. In that sense, they produce homogenous cheese that keeps for much longer but contains far less flavour and character. The unique quality of the milk is preserved during the raw milk production process. The quality is determined by factors such as the terroir and climate and can vary daily. Consumers need to understand that cheesemakers who don't pasteurise their milk must take far greater care to keep it uncontaminated than cheesemakers who pasteurise their milk. As a result, artisan cheesemakers often have to adjust the cheesemaking process, which requires extra attention and expertise and frequently brings some headaches along with it. In that respect, producing raw milk cheese is a daily challenge that people cannot simply leave up to machines. And that's precisely what gives raw milk cheeses their unique and artisanal character. In my opinion, choosing pasteurised milk is purely a matter of convenience: as a farmer, when you process raw milk, you need to work in extremely hygienic conditions. If you don't, your milk will cause all sorts of problems, and if you don't pasteurise that milk, those problems will transfer to the cheese.

The flavour of the cheese continues to be the definitive element, but the background information about the cheese is becoming increasingly essential. That's what inspired us to create this book; to help people understand the fascinating and highly diverse world of real cheese and the difference between the cheese found on supermarket shelves and cheese made on small-scale farms.

TASTING IS ONE OF THE ESSENTIAL TASKS OF AN AFFINEUR, SO I HAVE QUITE A FEW CHEESES UNDER MY BELT.

———

AFFINAGE, A LIVING CRAFT

A cheese affineur ensures that cheeses mature optimally. And this process starts with cheese selection. We consider several aspects when making this selection:
- *Artisanal cheese:* cheeses made on an industrial scale are off the table
- *Farmhouse cheese:* we like to work with cheeses where the fresh milk is processed at the farm
- *Raw milk:* we work as much as possible with cheeses made from raw milk, and at least 80% of our assortment consists of raw milk cheeses
- *Summer milk:* whenever we can, we work with cheeses made from spring or summer milk when the animals can graze outside

The affinage or maturing of raw milk cheese is not a science; it's a craft. As an affineur, I buy a living product to which I add value: raw milk cheeses are not restricted to a firm set of rules. Sometimes a cheese that comes in later can mature more quickly than a cheese brought in

earlier. That's why we don't work with the first in, first out principle. We closely follow the progress of every cheese that comes in.

Every morning, I touch and smell the cheeses to see how they're evolving. Based on my findings, we turn, wash or adjust the temperature, humidity or ventilation to provide as consistent a product as possible. An artisanal cheesemaker or cheese affineur strives to develop a consistently high-quality product. But this is a utopia, and the fascinating challenge lies in delivering an artisanal product at a consistently high level every day. In that regard, craftsmanship is just as crucial for affineurs as for cheesemakers. We need to have the same qualities. Craftsmanship isn't old-fashioned and dull, it's an exhilarating and highly personal process.

Patience is an essential quality, and we must respect tradition while not losing sight of opportunities for innovation. That's why we look for artisanal producers who work in the same vein; people who, with their tremendous effort and dedication, should be justifiably proud of their products. We also like to draw attention to those craftsmen by providing enriching information about their products because we must give credit where credit is due. As an affineur, cheesemonger and exporter, I consider it a privilege to contribute to this appreciation of the craft.

When we moved to the De Koninck brewery site, we consciously created nine different ripening spaces, where we can mature each variety of cheese in the appropriate atmosphere and develop their flavours and aromas under ideal conditions.

MY TOP THREE BELGIAN CHEESES

As I mentioned earlier, I wasn't much of a cheese fan as a child. However, once I had tried my first delicious cheese, I acquired a taste for it, and soon I discovered that I liked all kinds of cheese. Today, when someone asks me what my favourite cheese is, I always give a

diplomatic answer: every cheese has its moments. And I really do believe that is the case. Also, when someone asks me if I eat cheese every day, my answer is a resounding yes. Many of my customers from the restaurant trade give me an odd look when I order a cheese plate after the main course. Tasting is one of the essential tasks of an affineur, so I have quite a few cheeses under my belt.

Personally, I'm a huge fan of young, elegant, yet flavourful fresh cheeses, such as a delicious buffalo mozzarella, Burrata or buffalo ricotta, which I regularly use when I'm cooking at home.

As far as "table cheese" goes, I prefer more pronounced cheeses: red-smear and blue cheeses head my list. A finely balanced Roquefort like those made by Le Vieux Berger or a lovely Stichelton is deliciously creamy and complex, and with the right drink to serve it with, you can make the most fantastic combinations.

1. Herve cheese from Madeleine Hanssen

If I'm allowed to choose my absolute favourite, I would choose Madeleine Hanssen's raw milk Herve cheese. The Herve is the only Belgian cheese with an AOP (*Appellation d'Origine Protégée*, or Protected Designation of Origin) designation.

The Herve is, like many AOP cheeses, strongly linked with the region (terroir) it comes from: it's made in eastern Belgium on the Plateau de Herve. People have tried to reproduce Herve cheese elsewhere but without success. Its location between the Meuse and the Vesdre rivers, where the *Brevibacterium linens* bacterium naturally occurs, gives the cheese its unique flavour. This cheese has been produced for over 800 years, and its sale in other regions has inspired other cheesemakers, for instance in the Alsace region and in Southern Germany.

There are several varieties: the *doux*, or soft variety, and the more pronounced *picant* version, which has the same base but is left to mature longer and is washed more frequently.

Despite its history and influence, it is a cheese that is only made by two producers today: Herve Societé, which makes the cheese from pasteurised milk, and Fromagerie du Vieux Moulin, which only processes raw milk. I personally love the combination of a Herve cheese with a glass of stout or a fruity wine from Alsace.

Herve cheese is also a perfect cheese for cooking. I have served it with leek and escargots de Namur, but it's also a perfect addition to a hearty *tartiflette*.

2. Cabriolait from Het Hinkelspel

Another one of my favourite cheeses is the Cabriolait from Het Hinkelspel, a cheese cooperative established in Ghent in the 1980s. Their story is just as unique as their cheeses. Three fellow students, Alexander, Jos, and Bart, wanted to produce real, raw milk cheeses. They were given a room in a beguinage in Ghent where they made their first cheeses. They soon moved to a larger space where they also set up a shop. They were pioneers in the production of organic milk: all their cheeses have been organic since 2001.

At first, Het Hinkelspel incorporated cow's milk into their cheeses but later also started including goat's milk. My personal favourite is a goat's milk cheese. If Belgium is known for any one type of cheese, it's their monastic cheese. Those typical semi-soft cheeses are no longer solely produced in monasteries. After years of making their Pas De Rouge, Het Hinkelspel has also developed a fantastic goat's cheese version of this classic: the Cabriolait. This cheese has a flavour that is perfectly balanced between the fresh goat's cheese and the lovely, full flavour of the *linens* bacteria.

3. OG Kristal

The OG Kristal has grown in recent years to become our most successful export product. And the story behind my first meeting with Johan, the cheesemaker, is worth telling. In 2011, my father published his first cheese and beer book together with beer sommelier Ben Vinken. They combined their expertise and wrote a book that paired 50 Belgian beers with 50 European cheeses. While making this book, we met a lot of people from the brewing world. One day, I received a call from Hans Depypere, the owner of the Sint Bernardus brewery. He told me about a cheesemaker from the Roeselare region who had developed a cheese with hop shoots, a Belgian delicacy. We were invited to the launch of this new cheese, and that's how we got to meet the makers behind the cheese: Johan and Dominique Deweer, makers of a highly diverse assortment of cheeses.

That evening, we were invited to stop by the dairy to discover some of their other cheeses.

We were immediately blown away by their Gouda-style crumbly cheese. After 20 months of maturation, this cheese still has a rich, creamy structure, combined with large crystals from the maturing process. Its flavour profile is highly umami with caramel and butterscotch tones. When I asked Johan how that came about, he

told me a funny anecdote: the cheese was the result of happy coincidence. Johan loves to experiment and is constantly trying out new recipes and techniques. While he was making a recipe for Gouda cheese, he decided to try something different (he still won't tell me what). When the cheese was old enough to be sold in the farmhouse shop as a young cheese, the cheese turned out to have an unpleasant texture. They didn't want to sell the cheese, but they felt it was a waste to throw it away, so they decided to keep it for personal consumption. Because they had made a whole batch of the cheese, it took a while before they had finished it all; and as time went by, they discovered that the cheese matured really well. Thankfully, Johan had jotted down his "bad" recipe, and since then, he has been making OG Kristal in precisely the same way. We want to share this unique Belgian cheese with the rest of the world, so we're staunch champions of promoting this cheese.

EXPERIMENTATION AND EXPORT

Making artisanal cheese is a real challenge. And because I have been closely involved in the cheesemaking process as a partner for several years, I realise that only too well. Some cheesemakers, both newcomers and established names, ask me which cheese varieties are still in demand. They want to know where potential opportunities lie. It makes sense that a farmer wants to create added value with their dairy products.

I still see room for a blue cheese, a cheese variety for which Belgium already has an excellent reputation. And I've personally spent the last two years searching for a Belgian version of the French Époisses cheese. Together with Smaakhoeve De Lochtenberg and Filliers, we're close to creating a gin-based Époisses-style cheese. It's a complex process, both in terms of flavour and texture, which will serve to inspire other cheesemakers. Together, we taste to see how we can optimise the flavour and texture of such a cheese, so we can enrich the Belgian cheese landscape even further and add to its distinctiveness. The aim is to introduce something new and innovative and thereby further expand the assortment of Belgian cheeses for the international market.

As an exporter, I feel it is my duty to help Belgian producers flourish and promote their cheeses. We don't have any major cheeses with appellation designations as they do in France or Italy, but that doesn't have to be an impediment. What we do have in this country are diversity and individuality. And, with such a unique flavour profile, we can often fill a gap in the market. The hardest part is bringing people from outside of the country into contact with an unfamiliar Belgian cheese. However, once they've had a taste, they quickly come round and turn out to be loyal customers. We always look for typical Belgian artisan cheese because that's what cheesemongers abroad are looking to buy. Of course, this will always remain a niche product. A small artisanal producer in Belgium can never meet the total market demand in a country like the United States. That's why we focus on high-end shops specialising in niche products.

We take tremendous pleasure not only in seeing our Belgian cheeses appear on the menu at top-class restaurants but also in high-end speciality shops across the globe. But it doesn't end there: we discovered that a cheese shop in Houston has sent our cheeses to the International Space Station twice. The sky is no longer the limit!

A CHEESE SHOP IN HOUSTON HAS SENT OUR CHEESES TO THE INTERNATIONAL SPACE STATION TWICE. THE SKY IS NO LONGER THE LIMIT!

TASTE PROFILE

HERVE PIKANT
La Fromagerie du Vieux Moulin

Soft Belgian PDO cheese made from cow's milk with a washed rind

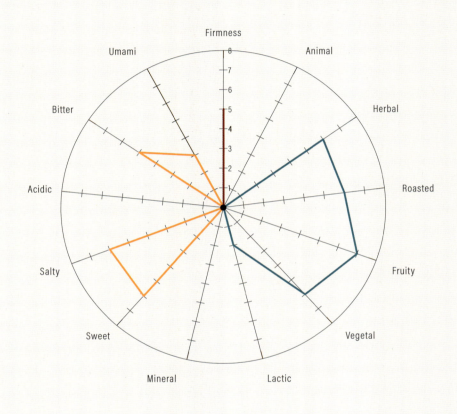

TEXTURE	**SOFT, SPRINGY AND SUPPLE**	
DOMINANT FLAVOURS	**FLOWERS**	
	NUTS	
	HAY, GRASS	
	HERBS	
SUBTLE NOTES	**COFFEE**	
	GRAPEFRUIT	
WINE TIPS	**SWEET WHITE WINE FROM LATE HARVEST GRAPES**	
	e.g. type Spätlese (Riesling)	
	HIGHLY AROMATIC WHITE WINE	
	e.g. Gewürztraminer	

TASTE PROFILE

CABRIOLAIT
Kaasmakerij Het Hinkelspel

Belgian semi-hard goat's cheese

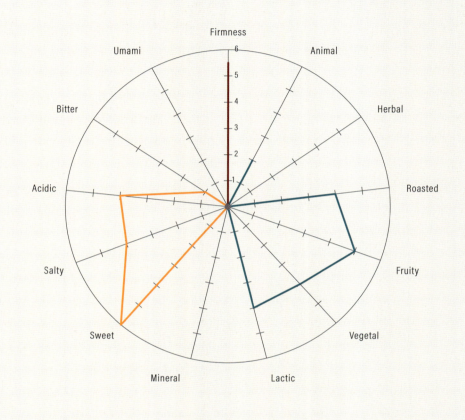

TEXTURE	**SEMI-HARD, SUPPLE AND CREAMY**
DOMINANT FLAVOURS	**HAZELNUTS**
	HAY, STRAW
	TOASTED BREAD, ROASTED NUTS
	YOGURT
SUBTLE NOTES	**GRAPEFRUIT**
	BARNYARD
	BUTTER
WINE TIPS	**FRESH WHITE WINE, WHETHER OR NOT WITH GRASSY OR GREEN AROMAS**
	e.g. Chardonnay without wood ripening or Sauvignon Blanc

REMEKER
working with nature

CHEESEMAKER

JAN DIRK VAN DE VOORT
Remeker
Founded in 1985
Lunteren, Gelderland
THE NETHERLANDS

WWW.REMEKER.NL

BECAUSE OF ITS UNIQUE FLAVOUR, JERSEY MILK STANDS OUT FROM THE ORDINARY MILK PRODUCED BY MAINLY BLACK AND WHITE COWS. I WANTED TO MAKE USE OF THAT DISTINCTIVE FLAVOUR TO MARKET MY OWN DAIRY PRODUCT.

CHEESE TRADITION

The Netherlands has a long-standing tradition when it comes to making cheese. The Low Countries are primarily composed of peatlands that can be best exploited by growing grass. Cows have always been kept in the western and northern parts of the country, where peat soil has been prevalent. A livestock farmer would historically have had about eight dairy cows; the raw milk provided by these cows was processed at the farm into butter or cheese. Until the Middle Ages, this was mostly soft cheese; after this period, primarily hard cheeses were produced because of their longer shelf life.

Today, the average livestock farmer in the Netherlands has 100 dairy cows and practically all the milk is processed in cooperative dairy factories. Over half of the milk produced by these 16,000 livestock farmers is pasteurised and processed into cheese; the rest is converted into numerous processed dairy products. A small portion of the milk is still processed at the farm itself. Approximately 400 farmers personally process all their milk into farm cheese. You will find these farmers mostly in the western part of the Netherlands.

BREAKING WITH TRADITION

Our business is located in the central Netherlands, in the Gelderse Vallei (Gelderland Valley). Our farm is named the Groote Voort and has been the property of the Van de Voort family since 1600. My grandparents made their own cheese from the milk produced by our black and white cows up until the cooperative was founded and all the farmers in our area stopped making butter and cheese. All that is left of our farm's cheesemaking days are the traditional cheese knife and a small cheese cave with curing tubs; the family's cheesemaking expertise was never passed down.

My father inherited a mixed-use farm from his father. He was the first "real" farmer in the family. My forefathers were more like managers and left the actual farm work to their personnel. My father studied to become a farmer and even went on a study trip abroad to the US, where he worked with Jersey cows for the first time. It was an experience that left its mark on the rest of his life. When the EEC, the predecessor to the EU, was formed, it became possible to import other breeds in addition to the Netherlands' traditional breeds. My father took the opportunity and became the first livestock farmer in the Netherlands to import Jersey cows, first from Germany and later from Denmark.

Ever since I was a young boy, I knew I wanted to become a farmer, and so I studied agriculture. My agriculture degree focused on intensive farming with maximum yields. When I returned to the farm and started working together with my father to shape the business, we doubled our livestock population to 130 Jersey dairy cows and said goodbye to the chickens and pigs. After a couple of years of intensive farming in the early eighties, with large quantities of fertilizer, feed concentrates and high levels of milk production, this type of farming lost its appeal for me.

Because of its unique flavour, Jersey milk stands out from the ordinary milk mainly produced by black and white cows. I wanted to make use of that distinctive flavour to market my own dairy product. I started out by making butter but I quickly turned to making raw milk cheese. It was very small-scale at first; everything was done by hand and with simple, borrowed cheesemaking equipment. The flavour of those first homemade cheeses was truly distinctive, and I sold the cheeses at farmers' markets. I briefly experimented with a soft, red-smear cheese, but we were not given permission to make this type of cheese. And so, I focused on hard cheese variations of the Gouda recipe.

THE BIRTH OF REMEKER

The farm is situated on grassland with a gorgeous centuries-old hedgerow called Remeker. The name dates from 1600 and the property has always belonged to the family. You can break the name down into "reem", which means bordered, and "eker", a traditional word for oak; in other words, a field surrounded by oak hedgerows. After a year of cheesemaking, we decided to name our cheese Remeker.

Our cheese recipe developed over time. We wash the curds, which classifies the cheese as a Gouda cheese; however, other than that, the way we make cheese is not at all similar to the farmers who make "farm cheese" in the western part of the country. We cut the curds into tiny pieces, as is done in the making of mountain cheese. The curds are only washed once and they are not heated, keeping all the enzymes in the curds intact. During the entire cheesemaking process, the temperature does not exceed 38°C, the body temperature of a cow.

We must have spent over ten years of trial and error perfecting a recipe suitable for our rich milk with its high fat content and protein levels until the cheese had its own characteristic taste. From the beginning, I made cheese without using saltpetre as a preservative. We brought endless batches of cheese away to be melted over the years and managed only to lose money during this period. But I was determined to master the art of cheesemaking, and every successful batch of cheese that tasted good was worth the setbacks. I know all about the pitfalls and shortcomings in cheesemaking because I had experienced first-hand all the things that went wrong in the cheese we produced.

In the early nineties, we transformed our business into an organic farm and cancelled our membership to the dairy cooperative. All our milk was converted into cheese, which we did four times a week. The milk harvested the previous day was cooled and that morning's milk went straight into the cheese vat. The organic shops valued our cheese and paid us enough to cover our costs. The lesser quality cheeses were also sold, and that is how we finally started making a profit producing cheese on our farm. We gradually built up our Remeker brand in the organic farming world in the Netherlands, Germany and Belgium; it is an organic, raw milk, Jersey cheese with the wax rind typical of practically all Dutch cheese. Many cheesemakers would be content with this result, but we were far from satisfied. In 2004, we turned our entire business upside down, starting with the cow.

RETHINKING THE BUSINESS

There were a couple of reasons why we wanted to embark on a new adventure. One important reason was that my wife, Irene, got involved with the business for a few years, and that led to quite a few fresh insights. Together we decided to stop using antibiotics to treat infections in the animals. Despite having worked organically for 15 years, we still regularly had cows with udder sores and claw lesions and sometimes calves with pneumonia. Everyone who was involved with our business wanted to know how we were going to resolve these issues without antibiotics. What we would do when an animal had an infection? We immediately started giving our animals feed that would be broken down in the rumen and not, as is usually done, feed that is broken down further along in the digestive tract. In practice, this means that the animals were no longer given maize silage or concentrate pellets in their feed, only grass products. The best reflection of how the cow feels about it is her fresh manure. Feed her grass products and she will give you finely digested manure that smells of grass and sticks to your fingers like a salve in return. It did, however, result in a 30% reduction in the milk production and this was hard to take for our colleagues. The cheese batches were significantly smaller, but the cows were showing us in every way imaginable that we were on the right track. The number of infections declined, and the animals were much more active.

From that moment onwards, we started listening to and working with nature. The female calves were allowed to remain with their mothers. If I was too quick to remove a female calf from her mother, the next morning she would be back in the field – while I was asleep, Irene would put the calf back with her mother. Normally speaking, calves are disbudded once they are a few weeks old. We decided to stop disbudding calves and had two years to make our accommodations suitable for horned animals. Fully grown animals with horns do not fit in freestall barns, because a horned cow can seriously injure the cow standing in the adjacent stall because she cannot exit the stall. We decided to save some money and design a barn using our existing accommodations. We did so by getting the animals themselves involved. What sort of a barn would horned animals like? The result was a round, deep-litter barn, the first round barn in the Netherlands.

WORKING WITH NATURE'S FLAVOURS

We work with "natural sustainability" in mind, something we are only too happy to explain to anyone who visits our farm. We quickly discovered that we were still using substances such as insecticides and wormers that were anything but sustainable. Could we also survive without these substances if it came down to it? We did not know anyone who had any experience with this until we came across Hubert, a herbalist who lived just across the border in Germany. Hubert taught us about the beneficial impact of herbs. We started feeding the animals with a mixture containing approximately 40 different

WHAT DOES ALL THIS HAVE TO DO WITH A DISTINCTIVE, FLAVOURFUL CHEESE? EVERYTHING!

types of herbs that they liked to eat. The herbs ensured that worms were unable to grow in our animals. The herbs also supported their liver function, which enabled the animals to manage diseases much better due to their strong immune systems. We had plenty of herbs on our lands, but with this mixture, we have been working for over 10 years without wormers. Together with Hubert, we then developed a natural vitamin and mineral mixture that included dried fruit instead of synthetic minerals.

The land surrounding the farm was 100% grassland that had not been ploughed in 31 years. The animals maintain the fields and the grass looks better and better every year. Measurements have shown that not only the number of earthworms but also the number of bacteria and moulds in the soil continues to grow. We also see an increase in the humus content (carbon sequestration). The movement of earthworms penetrates and breaks down hydraulic barrier layers in the soil, allowing roots

to grow deeper and survive drought in the summer as well as preventing the soil from becoming saturated during the wet winters.

What does all this have to do with a distinctive, flavourful cheese? Everything! For us, the soil is the foundation and an essential part of our business' sustainability cycle. The soil is still very much undiscovered territory in scientific terms; it challenges us to push back boundaries. For instance, can we leave even more of the soil maintenance up to the animals? The answer is yes. As of last year, we took the step of letting our dairy cows eat 100% fresh grass and getting them out into the fields very early in the season. As far as we know, there are only a couple of farmers in the Netherlands who do this, but we hope that many more will follow in the years to come. In the winter, the animals are still given a small amount of crushed grains, together with silage and hay. In mid-March, when there is still little grass in the fields, the cows head outside for the first time. After ten days, the dairy cows have sufficient bacteria in their rumen to be able to digest fresh grass so they can start eating 100% fresh grass. At that point, the animals do not receive any additional feedstuffs, not even hay or grains. In the fields, we have troughs where the cows can feed on herbs, vitamins and minerals for supplemental feeding and self-medication. The dairy cows graze in expansive fields to which they return every other day. The grass remains short, and they graze on the grass that has grown in a couple of days. The manure and urine end up in the fields, and a local colony of rooks conveniently tears everything apart again in their search for dung beetles. We make the best cheeses from spring to the summer solstice, the time of year when the dairy cows only eat fresh grass. Most of this cheese is fermented into Olde Remeker.

The soil forms the basis, but what the animals eat significantly determines the texture and flavour of the cheese. Grass and herbs are ideal for this. Silage and concentrates are less suitable due to the proportions of omega-6 and omega-3 fatty acids in the feed. The closer the proportion between these substances in the feed that the animals receive, the closer this proportion will be in the milk that they produce. You can measure the aroma in milk, which indicates that the aromatic sub-

> FOR MANY YEARS, WE COATED OUR CHEESES WITH A PARAFFIN WAX COATING. THIS IS A SYNTHETIC COATING THAT ENSURES THAT THE CHEESE REMAINS FREE FROM MOISTURE AND IS PROTECTED FROM CHEESE MITES.

stances are stronger and more prevalent in milk that has equal proportions of these fatty acids. Horned animals increase this effect; the milk from these animals has the best fatty acid composition. Moreover, milk from grass-fed animals is more yellowish in colour and has a softer texture. However, the cows' milk yield is lower when they are dependent on only grass and herbs. You also need to breed cows that can eat 100% grass. We did this by keeping the bulls from our oldest animals that have proven that they can manage our new feeding system and having them breed with our livestock. The next generation is then better suited to thrive on the 100% grass feeding system.

HOME-FIELD ADVANTAGE

This is how the soil-grass-cow-manure-earthworm cycle does its work on our farm, almost unhindered by unnatural means. Besides earthworms, you will also find countless moulds, yeasts, and bacteria in our soil that are specific to our farm. They are accustomed to this cycle and will not be able to convert manure from another cycle as efficiently because they will not recognise it. The dairy cows lie in the fields in the summer and in the hay stall in the winter, fed by the manure that the animals themselves have produced from the silage from the fields. The moulds, bacteria, and yeasts travel through the cycle via the teats of the dairy cows. During milking, we only use a teat towel to remove dirt from the teat, leaving enough micro-organisms behind to pass on into the milk. The milk from our dairy cows is not heated during the cheese preparation process, not even the curds. The temperature of the milk and curds does not rise above the natural body temperature of the cow (38°C), leaving the micro-organisms intact.

For many years, we coated our cheeses with a paraffin wax coating. This is a synthetic coating that ensures that the cheese remains free from moisture and is protected from cheese mites. This coating works well in the efficient cheesemaking system ubiquitous in the Dutch agriculture and dairy industry. Our search for a different solution started when we stopped using antibiotics. We felt increasingly uncomfortable using paraffin wax. But our search for a natural rind alternative was not an easy journey. Tried and trusted methods did not work well at our farm for some reason or another. Then we came up with the idea of coating our cheeses with ghee, clarified butter used in India's cooking tradition. We took this idea and continued to develop and improve upon it. We now make ghee from the fat in our own whey. The whey from the cheese contains 10% of the original milk fat, which we extract using a centrifuge. We use this cream to make butter which, in turn, is used to make ghee. Two-thirds of the ghee is collected in glass jars and sold as cooking fat. We use the remaining third to coat our cheeses. After three weeks of coating, the microflora starts doing its work; they have come a long way via the cow's teat and can now grow on the cheese crust, feeding off the last sugary remains of the whey and salt that are still present on the crust. The yeasts go to work first and prepare the acidity (pH) of the rind surface for the moulds. Not long after that, you can clearly start to smell the white moulds. These moulds create enzymes which, in turn, break down the ghee. The ghee is converted into flavourings which migrate into the cheese. We discovered this method through research together with the University of Wageningen. We call it our home-field advantage.

EVERY CHEESE DESERVES ITS OWN (RIPENING) SPACE

We ripened our first natural rind cheeses in a ripening warehouse which was initially made for coated cheeses. The warehouse was made from concrete and plenty of insulating material. After a couple of years, we developed a whole new ripening space for our natural rind cheeses. Taking our own ghee-encrusted cheese as a starting point, we soon discovered that the space had to be made from natural materials, with a humidity level of 90% and a temperature of 16°C. The process behind it was like the process we used when constructing the round barn, except this time we looked at things from the cheese's vantage point. The humidity is provided by the groundwater – we live in a valley – in cellars under the cheese racks. We have two stories for the ripening of the cheese and a climate control unit at the highest point in the warehouse. This unit maintains the climate, filters the air, and provides gentle circulation within the space. There is nothing like that delicious smell that the microorganisms release in our ripening warehouse. And when you realise that all this comes from our own soil, it makes it even more special. In fact, every farmer can create their own distinctive cheese because each farm has a different soil and billions of different microorganisms to choose from in making their cheese. Research at the university has shown that approximately 40% of the aromatic components in cheese are created and determined by these microorganisms.

TOGETHER STRONG

A few years ago, my son Peter decided to get involved with the family business, with great success. He feels completely at home among the cheeses and the animals. Much to our delight, we have been making top cheese for over two years, and that has never happened before in my entire cheese career. Peter and I have a great team working with us, of course. We now have 90 Jersey dairy cows and we work with four other full-time employees. We have always stuck to using natural processes and, as a result, we have had to face big challenges several times in the past. Every time we managed to come up with a solution to those challenges, often solutions that nature herself provided. Making our customers a part of this adventure is a great way of helping us get through the hard times. We have an open culture and gladly share our expertise. We regularly make short videos of everything that goes on here, so customers are aware of what is happening at the farm. At the end of the day, our cheese is valued at its worth and we collaborate with fantastic buyers who enjoy working with us and with our cheeses. Peter has a talent for assessing cheese quality and loves to talk shop with our buyers.

We are all in this together: the consumers, the retailers, the restaurants and everyone at this farm. Together, we can enjoy an amazing cheese that is the result of our respect for nature and for all living beings both above and below ground.

TASTE PROFILE

REMEKER
Boerderij De Groote Voort

Dutch semi-hard cheese made from Jersey cow's milk

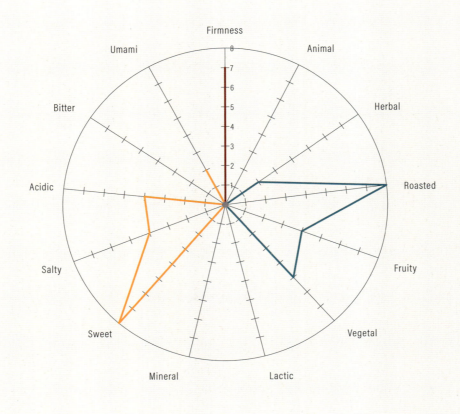

TEXTURE	**FIRM AND SMOOTH**
DOMINANT FLAVOURS	**TROPICAL FRUIT (PINEAPPLE)**
	NUTS
	BUTTER
SUBTLE NOTES	**YEAST**
	EARTHY TONES
	HUMUS
WINE TIPS	**AROMATIC HIGH-ACIDITY WHITE WINE**
	e.g. Riesling or Sauvignon Blanc

WRÅNGE-BÄCK

remaking the oldest cheese brand in Sweden

CHEESEMAKER

THOMAS BERGLUND
Almnäs Bruk
Founded in 1225
Hjo, Västergötland
SWEDEN

WWW.ALMNAS.COM

BRINGING THE OLDEST CHEESE BRAND BACK TO SWEDISH TABLES WAS A GREAT START, BUT WE DIDN'T STOP THERE.

CHEESE CULTURE IN SWEDEN

Swedish cheese culture is firmly rooted in our agrarian history. With a sparse population scattered across the country, cheese production remained a local enterprise for centuries. Farmsteads and small dairies supplied farmhands, villagers and the local priest with their version of a traditional hard cheese. Without the large cities of continental Europe that encouraged mass production, Swedish cheese evolved as artisanal treasures that varied from farm to farm.

But the rise of industrialization and a growing urban population – Stockholm tripled in size between 1850 and 1900 – heralded a change in our cheese culture. During this time, larger cheese producers looked to the continent for inspiration and began making Swedish versions of the great European cheeses such as Tilsiter and Emmentaler. These found a market in Stockholm and Gothenburg. However, after the Great Depression in 1929, Sweden's politicians sought a way to help farmers by collectivizing food production. It was the beginning of the food industry in our country, with its long-term consequences of making farmers financially dependent on large cooperatives and reducing food diversity. As smaller cheesemakers found it impossible to compete with large cooperatives who were protected by favourable legislation, Swedish independent cheeseries dwindled from approximately 800 in the early 1900s to less than 20 by the 1980s. And as generations of consumers grew accustomed to shopping for standardized food products in supermarkets, they lost a vital connection to the farmers who worked the land. To a large extent, the story of our farm followed this trajectory.

ALMNÄS, A HISTORIC SWEDISH FARM

Founded in 1225, Almnäs is a 3,580-hectare farm in the shire of Västergötland in central Sweden. It has produced cheese consistently since at least the 1500s, with deliveries to Swedish troops documented in the mid-1700s. Production increased in 1859 when a new cheesery was built at a tenement farm on Almnäs called Wrångebäck. Our archives still contain the diplomas awarded to the women cheesemakers at Wrångebäck for their talents in the dairy. However, the cheese from the farm really came into its own when Almnäs changed hands in 1887. The new owner, Oscar Dickson, saw Wrångebäck's potential and registered the name. Thus, Almnäs came to own the oldest cheese brand in Sweden. In fact, Dickson was so

taken with the cheese that he commissioned the architects of the Grand Hotel in Stockholm to construct a new cheesery at Almnäs. It was completed in 1892, and Wrångebäck grew in renown at country fairs around Sweden, eventually becoming the archetype of the classic Swedish Manor Cheese.

The brand's longevity means that Wrångebäck features in a few interesting moments in Swedish history, all documented in the farm's archives. In 1896, the cheese was served at the farewell dinner for the Swedish balloonist, Salomon August Andrée, the night before his ill-fated flight to the North Pole. In 1935, guests at the 500th anniversary dinner of the first Swedish parliament enjoyed Wrångebäck cheese. And a year later, Crown Princess Sibylla requested Wrångebäck for a charity event at Haga Castle in Stockholm.

When my great grandfather, Sanfrid Berglund, took ownership of Almnäs in 1915, this was our heritage. By 1946 we had four full-time cheesemakers producing Wrångebäck with milk from our cows. However, we were unable to increase production because laws favouring larger dairy cooperatives meant we couldn't buy milk from other farms. In 1961, my father made the decision to stop cheese production at Almnäs. However, we continued to produce milk for the big cooperatives, maintaining a herd of 800 Holsteins.

CHARTING A NEW COURSE IN SWEDISH CHEESEMAKING

When I said the story of Almnäs follows the history of cheesemaking in Sweden, I left out the last 33 years, which form a new chapter in our farm's history. In 1988, my siblings and I stepped into the role of running the family farm, and I became the managing director. We wanted to contribute in some way to the centuries of agriculture, animal husbandry, forestry, and industry that coloured the farm's long history. The first step was to become a certified EU-organic dairy, which we accomplished in 1999. We didn't realize it at the time, but this was hugely important for the future of Almnäs. Seven years later, my siblings and I decided to honour the farm's heritage by revitalizing our cheese production. And, of course, we began with the cheese that made our name: Wrångebäck.

Looking back, I didn't know what we were getting into, but from the outset, I was determined to remain true to traditional Swedish cheese production. I didn't want to continue simply producing milk for large dairy cooperatives. For me, it was very much about independence and freedom from a market system that destroys rural development, wreaks havoc on the land, and treats animals like commodities. We would make cheese in a way

that we could ideologically and philosophically defend. We would control the entire cheesemaking process. And we would stay small and entrepreneurial, connecting directly with our customers.

But where to begin? We had our 800 Holsteins and 2,500 acres of organic fields, but no working cheesery. I had an MBA, and I loved running the family business, but I was no cheesemaker. I quickly realized that I needed to start networking. I remember I went up to Stockholm to meet the manager of the cheese counter at NK, a high-end Swedish department store. I produced a ledger from the farm that showed they had ordered Wrångebäck from us on April 23, 1920, and I said, "I can't see you've paid for it." He laughed so hard and we struck up a lasting friendship, the first of many as I went about building a valuable network of fellow cheese enthusiasts.

Next, I joined the Swedish Cheese Society, where I learned there was already a dedicated group of people who were beginning to revitalize our traditional cheese culture. There I met and hired our first cheesemaker, Elisabeth Andersson. And then something incredibly lucky happened. Through family connections, I learned that the last dairyman making cheese at Almnäs back in the 1960s was still alive. When we found 82-year-old Hans Stiller – with the recipe for Wrångebäck ingrained in his memory – we had a direct link to the past. We drove our milk to Elisabeth's farm in Falköping and she and Hans worked together to create the first few batches of Wrångebäck. While our history helped us with a story and a purpose, to reestablish cheesemaking at Almnäs we needed to understand technology. So, for the third time in the farm's history, a new cheesery came to life – this time in our old distillery, built in 1770. And just as Swedish cheesemakers in the last century turned to the continent for inspiration, we did the same. Although we had no intention of copying the great cheeses of the continent, we were eager to learn from Swiss experts – my mother is Swiss, and we spent many family holidays in Switzerland where we first tasted Gruyere and Emmentaler. So, it was natural for me to turn to Swiss cheesemakers for advice in the modern-day techniques of making artisan cheese and for help sourcing the right equipment. Here in Sweden, there was no equipment to be had on the scale we needed, such as a four- or five-thousand litre copper cheese vat, which is the size of an ordinary village cheesery in the alps.

So, our new cheesery ended up with a combination of state-of-the-art manufacturing and pressing equipment housed in our centuries-old distillery building – a perfect reflection of our goal to revive cheesemaking using original recipies while acknowledging the advances of modern technology. We took the wooden planks from

BY SHARING WHAT WE HAVE LEARNED IN THE SAME SPIRIT OF GIVING, WE HOPE TO CONTRIBUTE TO A GLOBAL CHEESE RENAISSANCE WHERE EVERYONE – CHEESEMAKERS, AFFINEURS, CHEESEMONGERS AND CONSUMERS – BENEFIT.

the old dairy and used them in our new cheese cellar. The original bacterial cultures that remained in the planks infuse our cheese with an aroma that provides an authentic historical note through an unbroken chain of cultures dating at least 150 years.

By now we had a new cheesemaker at the farm, Kerstin Johansson, an extremely talented professional who heads a team of dedicated people whose attention to detail and focus on quality is exemplary. Over in our renovated hay barn, 3,700 cheeses rest in 225 square metres of climate-controlled storage, presided over by Tommy Larsson, an excellent salesman who loves to tell our story to prospective customers.

Encouraged by our progress, my siblings and I decided to expand our cheese production. I must admit, we were also hedging our bets: if Wrångebäck didn't live up to our expectations, we would have other cheeses to offer. We ended up creating three more cheeses, each contributing their unique taste and story to our overall brand. We've been refining and perfecting these same cheeses since 2010.

Wrångebäck

Wrångebäck is a round cheese, weighing about 8 kilograms (18 lbs). We make the cheese according to the original recipie, even though it takes one and a half times more milk than our Almnäs Tegel cheese and twice the length of time to make. Instead of coating the cheese with wax, we wash the rind with salt water, which benefits the bacterial culture called Brevibacterium Linens and gives the cheese a lovely reddish hue. Wrångebäck is matured for 9 to 12 months at 11 degrees Celsius.

Almnäs Tegel

Almnäs Tegel (Almnäs Brick) is a hard-pressed "scalded" cheese, its square shape inspired by the handmade bricks manufactured at the farm from the 1700s to 1976. On the rind, we have made an imprint of a child's foot, a historical reference to the real footprints found in the brick floor in the attic of the manor house at Almnäs. Hundreds of years ago as the bricks for the house were drying in the sun, the farm workers' children ran over them, leaving their footprints. In the early 1950s, we introduced a new logo and from then on, every brick manufactured at Almnäs bore the imprint of a child's foot. We have continued that tradition for Almnäs Tegel.

Each cheese weighs approximately 22 kilograms (58 pounds). Washing the cheese in salt water, in the same manner as Wrångebäck, endows the rind with a rusty red colour, reminiscent of the bricks we made at Almnäs. The cheese is matured between 18 and 22 months. In 2018, Almnäs Tegel won fourth prize in the World Cheese Competition out of a field of almost 4,000 cheeses.

Anno 1225

This medieval-style cheese is crafted using a braided wicker cheese mold, following a local basket design made hundreds of years ago in Västergötland shire. Unlike our other cheeses, Anno 1225 – named after the year of the farm's founding – is not washed with salt water. It is aged in its own storage facility, where the local fungi and yeast cultures establish themselves freely on the surface to bestow the rind with a natural mold. All we do is turn the cheese every three days. After 5 to 7 months in the cellars.

Anno 1225 is ready, with a unique flora and fauna. Each cheese weighs 3 to 4 kilograms (7 to 9 pounds). Anno 1225 received a Gold Award at the Birmingham, England, World Cheese Awards in 2012.

Almnäs 1 Litre

This cheese commemorates a special event. On October 21, 2010, the Swedish Crown Princess Victoria and Prince Daniel visited Almnäs. We invited them to make the first of a new cheese conceived in their honour. After aging at our storage facilities, we sent the cheese to their home at Haga Castle in Stockholm (the very same place where her grandmother Crown Princess Sibylla served Wrångebäck in 1936).

We named the cheese Almnäs 1 Litre to reference a custom established at Almnäs where tokens could be bought at the office to be used as payment for milk in the cow stable. It is derived from the other classic Swedish cheese, called Prästost (Priest's Cheese), and has become popular as a milder cheese of 8 to 10 months maturity.

THE MAGIC OF MOSAIC

As we continue to evolve our cheese-making techniques at Almnäs, our appreciation grows for our land, the terroir that makes cheese produced at the farm unique. We feed our cows only what we grow on the farm, so when people ask what accounts for the identifiable flavour and aroma of an Almnäs cheese, we say it's all down to the "mosaic" theory of field vegetation.

Almnäs is situated on the slopes of a hill, along eight kilometers of the Lake Vättern shoreline. In fact, many of our fields were originally lakebed, leaving us a legacy of rich, organic soil. Yet, the composition of soil varies greatly from field to field, with different ratios of sand and clay, depending on how high up the slopes you go. We plant each field with red and white clover, legumes, and different grasses; however, encouraged by our organic environment, natural flora established itself as well. This natural flora differs depending on the soil type, so a mosaic of different vegetation has evolved across our farm. As our cows move from field to field, they ingest a slightly different meal each time.

How does this influence the taste and aroma of our cheese? Each grass, crop, herb, legume and weed lives in symbiosis with its own set of bacteria. As the cows graze in different fields, they pick up these different microbes, which find their way into the milk. The greater the complexity of the diet, the richer the flavour of the milk. When we use the milk to make cheese, these microbes help break down the protein and the fatty acids that constitute the solids in the milk. As the more complex compounds are split into their simpler components, aromas are freed that contribute to the taste of the cheese. The point is, the more variety of microbes you have contributing to this process in the milk, the more complex is the cheese. It's one reason why Almnäs produces cheese with a recognizably sophisticated aroma and taste, and why no two are exactly the same.

SWEDISH SLOW-FOOD RENAISSANCE

While our focus has been to develop and promote Almnäs and the cheese we make, I'm happy to report we are but one influencer in a growing national awareness of Swedish food and sustainable farming practices. Over the last couple of decades, cheesemakers and farmers have raised the profile of traditions in the Swedish countryside – and bridged the gap between city dwellers and farmers. We are proud to be a part of this movement.

Bringing the oldest cheese brand back to Swedish tables was a great start, but we didn't stop there. From the beginning, we believed that networking and promoting our cheese on an international scale would help raise the profile of our farm and increase our global market. And time has proven us correct. We were the first to export artisan cheese from Sweden, to take a Swedish cheese to exhibit in Hong Kong, and to participate in the Fancy Food Show in the United States. We were also the first to enter a Swedish cheese in the World Cheese Awards. When we received accreditation to sell our cheese in China, Swedish media reports of the event helped raise awareness for our Swedish colleagues to build on the movement. We have participated several times in the world's most prestigious cheese exhibition in Bra, Italy, which is organized by leading proponents of the global Slow Food Movement. It was exciting for us to participate as just one of many cheesemakers with the same drive to deliver authentic, local food to people interested in ethical, sustainable agrarian practices.

We started by selling to Swedish and European cheese mongers, then arranged to deliver to premium wholesalers, who were kind enough to introduce us to leading chefs in Sweden. These professionals used our cheese to create dishes in the "New Nordic Kitchen" culinary movement. We're thrilled that we are part of establishing a Scandinavian esthetic in food that's now recognized around the world. Today, we host chefs at Almnäs so they can see where the cheese comes from and immerse themselves in the ambiance of our centuries-old farm.

IT TAKES A VILLAGE

We have come a long way in the last three decades and the future looks bright. But our journey is far from over. As part of a global movement where farmers are producing high quality goods sustainably, we're continuing to develop ethical, sustainable farming practices for an increasing number of customers who care about the environment and good animal husbandry.

To that end, we have invested in a new robotic milking barn, which not only creates a better working environment for our staff but provides an optimal calving environment and a stress-free milking experience for the cows. They can wander into the milking stalls at will to relieve udder pressure. As a consequence, our cows are calmer and produce more milk. We're able to reduce the size of our herd by 30 percent and still be able to generate the amount of milk to meet our cheesemaking requirements. A nice side effect is that we are also able to lower the carbon footprint on the farm.

And in yet another nod to our continental colleagues, we are slowly transitioning from Holsteins to the Brown Swiss cow. The Holstein is a fantastic animal for producing a lot of milk, but they are not as robust as we would like, and they don't live as long as we would like. In concert with our goal to go small and aim for high quality, we are introducing the Brown Swiss to Almnäs because they are robust, live longer, and produce milk with a better protein quality for making cheese. We are excited to see how this new breed will further improve the taste and aroma of our cheese.

When I look back on the 13 years since we reintroduced cheesemaking to Almnäs, it's clear to me that we couldn't have done it without the help of family, friends, and colleagues from our international "cheese family." A big challenge when I started on this journey was to find people I could learn from, and in the end, they were indispensable to helping us achieve our dream. If I have learned anything about the international artisanal cheese community, it's that everyone knows that one plus one equals three, and that sharing is better than competing. Many people have helped me without asking for anything in return – Walter Räss and his Swiss colleagues who advised me about equipment; the French cheese exporter, Maison Mons, who sent samples of our cheese with their written recommendation to their customers. Our enthusiastic reception in the United States is due to the unflagging promotional efforts of Adam Moskowitz and his dedicated team at Columbia Cheese. I feel a great debt to the generosity of all the people who have helped us over the years. By sharing what we have learned in the same spirit of giving, we hope to contribute to a global cheese renaissance where everyone – cheesemakers, affineurs, cheesemongers and consumers – benefit.

So, I would say to anyone starting out: discover what your personal strengths are and be generous with them to others, because they will return the favour. And don't waste too much energy worrying about the seemingly insurmountable obstacles: just keep your eye on the horizon. And remember, that village it takes to make a cheese, it's closer than you think.

TASTE PROFILE

WRÅNGEBÄCK OST
(Ostfabrik) Almnäs

Swedish semi-hard cheese made from cow's milk

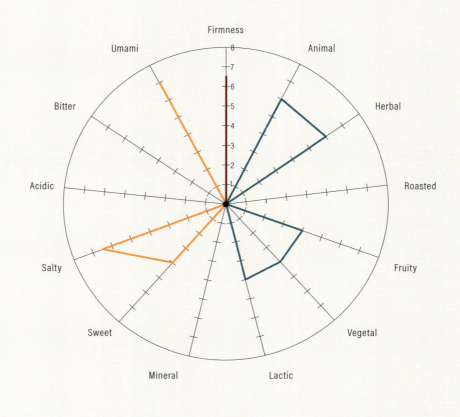

■ texture   ■ aroma   ■ flavour

TEXTURE	**SEMI-FIRM AND CREAMY**
DOMINANT FLAVOURS	**MEAT BROTH**
	BARNYARD
	MUSHROOMS
	NUTS
	SPICES
SUBTLE NOTES	**MILK, BUTTER**
	GRASS
WINE TIPS	**MUSCAT WINE**
	e.g. Muscat d'Alexandrie or Moscatel
	AGED RED WINE WITH TERTIARY AROMAS
	e.g. an aged Pinot Noir

74   ALMNÄS

CRAVERO
Parmigiano Reggiano with a heritage

CHEESE AFFINEUR

GIORGIO CRAVERO
Cravero Cheese
Founded in 1855
Bra, Piedmont
ITALY

WWW.CRAVERO-CHEESE.IT

IT WAS PROBABLY THE ROMAN CULTURE THAT DEVELOPED THE ART OF CHEESEMAKING AS WE KNOW IT TODAY.

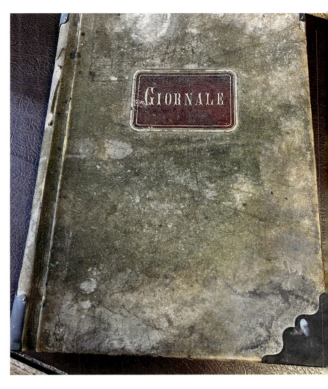

CHEESE HISTORY IN ITALY

Italy is home of the Roman Empire and great starter of the Renaissance in Europe, and its culture has flourished for centuries. Italy is commonly associated with art, music and gastronomy, but the cheese culture has also played and still plays a big part. History shows characters who witnessed the origin of cheese in Italy.

Cheese culture in Italy dates back to before the Roman Empire, and it was probably the Roman culture that developed the art of cheesemaking as we know it today. Among the many characters, Marcus Gavius Apicius, a gastronome, cook and Roman writer who lived during the reign of Tiberius sometime between the last century BC and the 1st century AD, is reputed to be the author of one of the oldest cooking treaties in the world, "de re coquinaria": ten books including 500 recipes. Marcus Gavius Apicius wrote extensively about the importance of cheese in the Roman diet and recipes.

Later, the ancestor of the mozzarella had been described for the very first time by Gaius Plinius Secundus. Plinio il Vecchio, in his *Naturalis historia*, a book about the whole

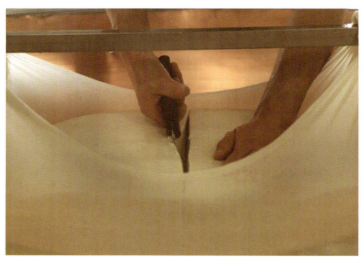

I DISCOVERED TO HAVE A PASSION FOR CHEESE SOMEWHERE IN MY SOUL THAT UNCONSCIOUSLY CAME OUT. MAYBE IT WAS WRITTEN SOMEWHERE, IN MY FIRST NAME FOR SURE.

of the natural world written from 77–79 AD, mentions the "laudatissimum caseum del Campo Cedicidio", a famous cheese coming from a place where the Basilicata region stands today. The cheese was definitely an ancestor of the well-known mozzarella, produced with cow's milk because there were no buffalos around then.

Regarding the Parmigiano Reggiano, historical evidence dates back to the Middle Ages. As the story goes, Benedictines and Cistercians monks, living in the Parma-Reggio Emilia region, decided to produce this kind of dry paste cheese in large wheels when they needed to find a way to increase the shelf life of the large quantity of milk they were producing. During the 1300s and 1400s, these monks had the monopoly on Parmigiano cheese and they began to trade it with other Italian regions. As the cheese became more popular, it spread to the rest of Europe.

By the early 14th century, Parmigiano had travelled from its place of origin in the Parma-Reggio Emilia region over the Appenini Mountains through Tuscany where ships departing from Pisa and Livorno carried it to other Mediterranean ports. The first recorded reference in 1254 documents that a noble woman from Genoa traded her house in return for an annual supply of cheese produced in Parma.
Back to the 13th century, there is the first evidence of a Caseus Parmensis trade, and then in 1351 the explicit mention of Boccaccio in The Decameron: "And there was a mountain all made of grated Parmigiano cheese, 'dwell folk that do nought else but make macaroni and ravioli, and boil them in capon's broth."

The idea and awareness of the PDO (protected designation of origin) concept dates from 1612 when the need to protect the Parma and Reggio Emilia cheeses from other similar cheeses led the Duke of Parma to make the designation of origin official with a certified deed. Despite wars in Europe that slowed down the production and export for a long period, the cheese gradually began to be exported in France, Germany, Holland and Spain. At the beginning of 1900 new skills such as the use of fermented whey and steam heating were introduced and are still crucial in the making of Parmigiano Reggiano.

The uniqueness of this cheese has reached its excellence since then and has remained unchanged. In fact, it is produced with the same ingredients – raw milk, rennet and salt – in the same artisanal way for about nine centuries to protect a genuine and natural production without any additive.
Today, Parmigiano Reggiano, produced by almost 300 dairies, is defined worldwide as the king of cheese. Because of that, Parmigiano Reggiano is widely imitated and rapidly becoming a commodity. It came to be an increasingly regulated cheese until 1934 with the foundation of the Consorzio del Pamigiano Reggiano.
From a legal point of view, since 1996, the name refers exclusively to the Parmigiano Reggiano PDO that identifies its production in a limited area in northern Italy, in five provinces to be precise: Parma, Reggio Emilia, Modena, Mantova to the right of the river Po, and Bologna to the left of the river Reno.
To identify the product as the authentic one, each wheel shows special and original marks: a casein plate with a unique and sequential alphanumeric code is applied for following its traceability and two different marking bands identify the dairy code and the month and year of production.
The minimum maturation age for a Parmigiano Reggiano wheel is 12 months at the dairy, the longest among all the PDO cheeses. After the 12th month each single wheel is carefully checked by the Consorzio del Parmigiano Reggiano experts to settle if it is worthy of his designated name and therefore continue the maturation up to 18, 24, 30, 36 months and more. The conforming wheels are marked with the fire-iron brand, thus becoming Parmigiano Reggiano.

CRAVERO, A FAMILY TRADITION

My family has been involved in cheese since 1855. Our family business was founded by my great-great-grandfather Giorgio, and it has grown through five generations and is currently led by me and my wife, Barbara.
Giorgio Cravero (1808–1882) and his son Giacomo (1856–1929) used to be either affineurs or cheese traders. Even my first couple of ancestors used to be Parmigiano Reggiano selecters and maturers and, at the same time, classic Italian cheeses traders. In our offices we keep their portraits and some leather covered registers that show nineteenth-century sales details like relics. Those figures testified that they marketed Parmigiano Reggiano, Gorgonzola, Fontina, Taleggio, the local Formaggio di Bra and butter as well.
Around one hundred years ago, my grandfather Giorgio (1890–1971), then in his thirties, became crucial for our family company because he was the man who decided to focus the whole business just on Parmigiano Reggiano. After the Second World War in the early 1950's, my father Giacomo, in his twenties, took over the family business when his father Giorgio retired because of heart problems. With the business devastated by the war and the crash of the prices, my father began to focus his efforts on the Italian market, losing the business's (few) foreign customers. In the following thirty years Giacomo's hard work established the Cravero Parmigiano Reggiano brand across the whole peninsula.
Jumping to today, I would say that I am an engaging and enthusiastic Parmigiano-Reggiano affineur, but I didn't grow up like that. When I was young I never thought about the family business, even if the Parmigiano

Reggiano smell was always in my nose and the maturation caves my second home.

When it was time to go to college I decided to study economics, but that didn't last long... One day (I was twenty and had just come back to Bra from Torino University) I told my parents during a family lunch that my career as a student was over. My relatives were shocked. A couple of days later my father suggested that l should spend some time with him visiting customers and producers. That suggestion was immediately successful because I discovered I had a passion somewhere in my soul that unconsciously came out. Maybe it was written somewhere, in my first name for sure.

A decade travelling up and down my country visiting customers and discovering new ones, I began to think outside the "Italian box". We used to sell almost exclusively in our country, but our Parmigiano Reggiano was, as far as I am concerned, one of the best, so why not try to go abroad to sell it?

Something crucial happened in 1997. We attended the very first Festival "CHEESE in BRA" organised by our hometown friends from Slow Food, the worldwide known grassroots organization, founded in 1989 in Bra to prevent the disappearance of local food cultures and traditions. Since then, we have never missed a single one of these festivals. Since the second festival in 1999 a substantial percentage of visitors have been cheese professionals from all over the world. We took advantage of their participation by showing them our caves, and at the same time I began to supply several reliable specialized cheese retailers and importers throughout all of Europe, the US, Japan and Australia. I have spent the last twenty years travelling and visiting my customers abroad for tastings and providing Parmigiano Reggiano culture education. I have also had the pleasure of fruitful and gratifying relationships.

During these trips, I gradually started to be aware of the positive "responses" to our tradition and our family business history, so I began to trust our Parmigiano Reggiano as something special. These interesting and exciting missions were successful: nowadays our company develops 80% of its turnover abroad, proudly distributing our Parmigiano Reggiano in around 20 countries.

Last but not least, can you guess my son's name? Giacomo, of course! He is a college student, and he is still figuring out what he will be as the sixth generation...

THE TERROIR

Since 1855 our family has been selecting and maturing the very best Parmigiano Reggiano. Our meticulous selection criteria, passed down through generations, together with a continuing respect for the traditions of our trade, help us to guarantee the quality we want.

Each cheese carries within it not only an individual flavour, but also the history of a land and its people's traditions: production and maturation techniques that are handed down from one generation to the next.

Our aim is to select the terroir and then select the cheeses. During the early '70s my father discovered the beautiful landscapes of Pavullo and Rubiera, mountains and foothills in the Emilia Romagna region. We still select our cheeses there in what we consider our "promised land". The total absence of pollution, the small-scale dairies and the rich and lush flora of that area allows the production of a very high quality milk.

Actually, these are places with a great variety of pastures where the cows eat local hay made of wildflowers, alfalfa, various herbs and grasses from unploughed meadows in season and the freshly cut grass in spring. Silage or fermented feed are neither allowed by the PDO nor by the tradition.

The cows are fed hay all year round to guarantee a constant level of milk quality. Hay is the forage that makes the majority of their diet and is supplemented with corn, barley, oat, rye and wheat. The local forage allows, through the cows' feed and resulting milk, a creaminess of the texture and a sweetness of the taste that identify the cheeses made in these areas.

Among the components of the terroir concept, the human relationships between producers and affineurs are fundamental. The casari (the cheesemakers) own essential and traditional skills and they work as their predecessors do, with care and passion. Using the word "terroir", I mean to have a very long and friendly relationship with farmers, trusting them and their job. I am proud to work with meticulous cheesemakers focused on the traditional practices and the qualities of the milk they produce from the farmers.

OUR METHOD OF AFFINAGE

Our careful cheese selection takes place at the producers' dairies, not before the cheeses are 12 months old. A member of our team taps every single wheel to identify those without defects that can proceed to the maturation process until the 24th month at least. After this crucial day, the "young" cheeses are ready to move from their birthplace in Emilia Romagna to our caves in Bra, located in the heart of the deep and rural Piemonte. Geographically, Piedmont indicates a region of foothills in a mountain range and in fact it is surrounded on three sides by the Alps. It borders with France, Switzerland and the Italian regions of Lombardia, Liguria and Valle d'Aosta.

Our facility in town is organised in the classic twenty-foot-high rooms with an allocation of five thousand wheels of Cravero Parmigiano Reggiano.

My father taught me (his father taught him like the previous 5 generations) that the time and attention we give to the care of these cheeses, and the close monitoring of the temperature and humidity of their environments, guarantee the unique nature of our product.

And so it is.

We love to describe our method of affinage as *natural*. In contrast to the majority of the Parmigiano Reggiano affinage sites, our secret touch lies in avoiding to heat the maturing rooms during the winter time. That way, during the cold winters in Piemonte, we let our cheeses "hibernate", and not dry them out. Since we select a creamy texture by terroir (do you remember?), it would be nonsense to "ruin" the cheese wheels during the second year of their lives.

We use an air conditioning system only from June to September. During the summertime we set a 24/7 temperature of 17°C/18°C and 70%/75% of humidity. On the contrary, in autumn, fall and winter the natural conditions guaranteed by the appropriateness of the ancient construction built during the 1700s keep the winter-time temperature between 6°C and 10°C with 70% of natural humidity.

We neither brush nor wash nor dry the wheels; the only mandatory procedure we need to follow is flipping them over every other week to ensure an even moisture distribution to maintain the softness of the texture and get the Cravero Parmigiano Reggiano ready to travel worldwide at its best age (24 to 30 months).

This way of affinage is pretty slow and gentle, no rushing, leaving the cheeses to dream on the shelves.

SOFT AND SWEET

We work with a handful of farms from the traditional designated Emilia Romagna region who, during the production process, pay particular attention to the succulence of their cheese texture by carefully handling the curd. This allows us to mature the wheels in a natural way and to reach the texture and profile test we are looking for and consider our mission: "soft and sweet".

Because we focus on aging wheels whose most important characteristics are the creaminess of the texture and the sweetness of the taste, we decided that in order to get a moist, creamy cheese, the pick of the maturation is from 24 months to 30 months. At that age the moist texture is interposed with the crunch of the tyrosine crystals.

Lactic, buttery, fruity, really savoury, is how we dream of it, the softer texture of the cheese helps the vivid flavours explode in your mouth. No bitterness damages its finish. Delicious.

I think that it's an exemplary eating cheese, a Parmigiano Reggiano that you can serve on a cheese board as *aperitivo*, accompanied by a glass of sparkling white wine.

Our Parmigiano Reggiano has its own strong identity. For nearly two centuries our family has endeavoured to pay tribute to this cheese and constantly tried to maintain the highest standards of quality while remaining faithful to authentic traditions.

NOT A COMMODITY

Around ten years ago, something happened when I was attending the world-famous Cheesemonger Invitational event in New York City, a unique competition that honours and emphasises the profession of the cheesemonger. It was almost midnight and euphoria, happiness and confidence filled the building. Hundreds of people were chatting cheese, drinking beer, dancing and pretending to change the world.

I was having a chat with an American cheesemonger when the concept of commodity popped up. A commodity is a product that is indistinguishable from ones manufactured or provided by competing companies and that therefore sells primarily on the basis of price rather than quality or style.

I was immediately blown away by the opposite of this concept and I decided to use the claim 'Not A Commodity' at once. Since then, the Cravero T-shirts 'Not A Commodity' are still in stock.

I think that this assertion is fit for each colleague of mine, the co-authors of this book. We want to save the world from commoditization, because terroirs are particular, skills and traditions are special and cheeses are unique. People have to be educated and we have to spread the word!

A COMMODITY IS A PRODUCT THAT IS INDISTINGUISHABLE FROM ONES MANUFACTURED OR PROVIDED BY COMPETING COMPANIES AND THAT THEREFORE SELLS PRIMARILY ON THE BASIS OF PRICE RATHER THAN QUALITY OR STYLE.

TASTE PROFILE | PARMIGIANO REGGIANO
Cravero

Italian hard, granular cheese made from cow's milk

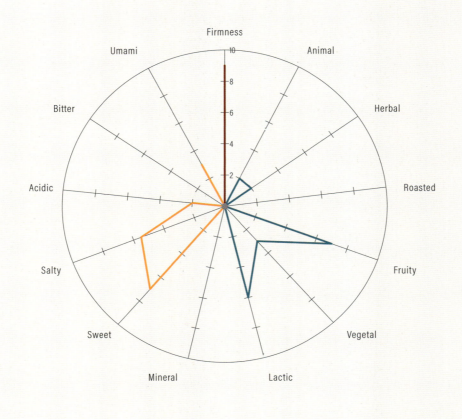

■ texture   ■ aroma   ■ flavour

TEXTURE	**FIRM AND GRAINY**
DOMINANT FLAVOURS	**TROPICAL FRUIT (PINEAPPLE)**
	NUTS
	YOGURT
SUBTLE NOTES	**HEATHER**
	GRASS
	MEAT BROTH
WINE TIPS	**MUSCAT WINE**
	e.g. Zibibibo or Muscat d'Alexandrie or Moscatel
	STRONG RED WINE
	e.g. Zinfandel, Montepulciano or Nebbiolo

FORMAGGI DEBBENE

organic
Pecorino
from Sardinia

CHEESEMAKER

GIANFRANCO EN SALVATORE BUSSU
Formaggi Debbene
Founded in 1971
Campeda plateau, Sardinia
ITALY

WWW.FORMAGGIDEBBENE.IT

AN AGROPASTORAL SYSTEM BASED ON SHEEP AND GOATS WAS PRESENT IN CENTRAL ITALY SEVERAL CENTURIES BC. COWS WITH THE PURPOSE OF CHEESE PRODUCTION ARRIVED CENTURIES LATER AND MAINLY IN THE NORTHERN PART OF THE COUNTRY.

THE IMPORTANCE OF PECORINO IN ITALY

Everything started approximately seven centuries BC in the central part of Italy, in the Tuscan-Roman Tirrenian coast, in particular, where there have been finds of primordial dairy technology. Probably this was the ancestor of Pecorino Romano – in fact, it has been proven that an agropastoral system based on sheep and goats was present in those centuries. Research supports the idea that cows arrived for the purpose of cheese production centuries later and mainly in the northern part of the country. Along the Italian peninsula even today, the animal milk's distribution follows the shape of nature: in the northern Alpine chain and plateau there are only cows and rarely goats, then in the irregular hilly and mountain territory of central and south Italy, including Sardinia and Sicily, we mainly have sheep and more recently buffaloes in Lazio and Campania. This has been facilitated by climatic conditions, which are more friendly to sheep in the southern part of the country. So there is a reason if nowadays the most famous Italian cheeses are produced with different kinds of milk: Parmigiano Reggiano, Grana Padano and Gorgonzola (cow); Pecorino Romano and Fiore Sardo (sheep); Mozzarella di Bufala (buffalo). It shows that we are part of a bigger picture, where Pecorino cheese is an important theme with various actors. In fact the term "Pecorino" only refers to a cheese made with sheep's milk, but it's extremely important to ask where the cheese comes from to estimate taste profiles and characteristics.

OUR PIECE OF HISTORY, WITH A TOUCH OF PASSION

We were children when our father and mother bought a piece of land in Campeda (Macomer), where our farm is built today, even if our family roots lie in Ollolai, in Barbagia, located in the centre of Sardinia. We belong to a family of shepherds, and we have always breathed the air of nature: we started milking sheep, twice a day, and making cheese with our father when we were 7 years old. We went to school until we were 16 and and always returned to the farm. When you run a farm there is always a task for everybody and never too many workers, so our father involved us either in herding, milking or cheesemaking and one day we realized he was preparing us to lead the farm in the future.

In June we used to participate in the shearing festival, an occasion to celebrate the end of the milking season and the beginning of the summer vacations. Unfortunately, the festival doesn't exist anymore – wool is no longer a source of income as in the old days and sheep are sheared by specialised teams in Australia or New Zealand. Mastering the art of herding and cheesemaking originated in a long tradition of experience, education and familiarity, and we can say we have been lucky enough to have all those sources of knowledge.

Approximately 20 years ago we started travelling and doing national fairs, expecially Cheese in Bra which gave us the possibility to present our Presidium Slow Food, Fiore Sardo DOP, but most of all reassured us we were steering our farm in the right direction: raw milk cheese production, absence of industrial starters in favour of natural ones, like natural whey, and protection of terroir. This event has pushed us to improve and continue in the same direction. In fact in 2019 our Fiore Sardo DOP was awarded "cheese of the year" at

the Italian Cheese Awards, and that has given us a lot of visibility.

The sense of belonging to our culture, the Sardinian one, has always inspired us. It's a millennial culture based on agriculture, pastoralism, cheesemaking and handcrafting and we have always felt the need to protect it, because we are part of its system of values. When we are asked where the passion for cheese comes from, we say: it's in our blood and we want to serve it with a great sense of respect. We try hard to express a full sense of nature in what we do: from feeding the sheep, which is done 100% in our pastures, to raw milk production, from natural smoking for Fiore Sardo DOP to a natural aging in our caves. For this reason too we have stuck to organic certification since the first years of this century. It's no matter of convenience, it's a belief that comes from the love of nature and that has helped us to give sense to our ancestral practices. As a result, consumers recognize our cheese as not only real, natural, but also as elegant, different and expressive of a terroir. Genuineness is what we are looking for, in all cheeses. For us, a genuine cheese is made by hand, with hard labour, coming from a raw material that has been respected and well treated. Real cheese is not artifacted and, most important of all, is made with unpasturised milk. Real cheese represents the producer, who he/she is, the choices, the attitude and even the characteristics of the pasture and of the real context where it comes from. Generally, behind each great cheese stands a producer who is a great person as well. This might sound a bit generic, but it expresses our belief that real cheese speaks the same language as the producer and the same language of the terroir. In one word: we have to get the terroir when we approach a cheese.

TRANSMITTING EMOTIONS AND PERPETUATING TRADITIONS

Recent sociological developments have transformed people's approach to gastronomy. We are moving from the need to eat to the need to have experiences through eating. People don't only have the need to have enough food but also to have good food. So imagine how this is changing the role of traditional cheeses in our food society – what an opportunity. This phenomenon has given us the chance to concentrate on our strengths: the capacity to generate emotions (people say our cheese is beatifully good) and extreme respect for traditional methods of herding and production. So our purpose is to perpetuate our strengths and Sardinian culture, which is very deep in our island. Even though we regret our Fiore Sardo DOP is not very well known in the region, it is very much appreciated in the rest of Italy and Europe.

This is confirmed by history: once upon a time, the Fiore Sardo was exclusively marketed on the continent, because it was not appreciated in Sardinia. Today one wonders how this is possible, but reviewing the story we came up with an idea. Originally, the Fiore Sardo was produced by shepherds during the grazing period. They spent the summer at 1000 meters above sea level in the areas surrounding Ollolai, the capital of Barbagia, the mountainous area of the central region of Sardinia. In November, they descended towards the sea and in April

they went back. Pecorino was produced in the "pinnettas" or "pinnettu", shelters with a circular stone base and a roof of branches and trunks inside which the shepherd produced pecorino. To warm up the milk they lit a fire. The heat was used to facilitate the formation of the "skin" (a light peel) and the smoke that invaded the shelter preserved the cheese from insects and excessive mold formation. During the winter period, when the wheels were dry enough to be transported, they were taken to the villages in the mountains, to the cellars of the shepherds' houses, where the women took care of them during the maturation until November, when it was time to take the road back to the sea. In this period, the traders went up one single time to buy all the produced cheese. Pecorino was therefore very seasoned, very salty and very smoked, ideal for consumers outside Sardinia, but way too strong to be consumed by Sardinians.

When the Consortium for the Protection of Fiore Sardo DOP was founded, numerous shepherds were present: over a hundred shepherds from the area joined. This shows the deep bond between Sardinia, the shepherds and the art of dairy farming. However, things have become increasingly difficult for the shepherds and the generational change is no longer taken for granted. This is why we resist and exist, to safeguard an ancestral method, a cultural system and artisan cheesemaking. This is why we love to explain how our cheesemaking method refers to history.

TRADITIONAL CHEESEMAKING METHODS

Fresh, raw milk from Sardinian sheep is placed in copper boilers and coagulated at an average temperature of 32°C to 35°C using lamb rennet, normally produced by ourselves. After 20 to 30 minutes, depending on the season, the curd is finely broken up to the size of a grain of rice and left to settle on the bottom. Then, without subjecting the mass to any type of cooking, it is patiently collected from the bottom of the boiler in pieces and deposited in the characteristic truncated cone-shaped molds called "pischeddas". At this point we hand press the wheel to obtain the maximum bleeding of the whey. When it is firm, the wheel is extracted and left to rest for about 24 hours, after which it is immersed in the brine, where each kilo of cheese generally remains for 8 to 12 hours. The cheeses then go onto a trellis of reeds

> WE ARE LUCKY TO DO A JOB THAT HAS EXISTED FOR THOUSANDS OF YEARS: WE ARE SHEPHERDS FIRST AND CHEESEMAKERS SECOND.

("sa cannizza"), usually near the fire, where they dry and smoke for about two weeks, continuously changing position to create an homogeneous level of smoking for each wheel. Finally, they are aged in a cool and dry environment, on the ground, where they remain for at least 105 days, which is the minimum to get the DOP, but we believe the best cheeses are reached at 5 to 6 months of maturation with winter milk. In fact, the cheeses produced in December and January with the fattiest milk reach the maturation of 5 to 6 months in summer, which is the ideal amount to appreciate a sweet product, persuasive, with notes of milk, butter and honey enriched with smoked notes that embrace the complexity of this magnificent cheese. In reality, there is another time of the year ideal for the purchase of Fiore Sardo DOP. It is months of September and October, but for the 10-month seasoned version. The fat keeps the texture soft, allowing the cheeses to be preserved at their best, even after many months, without ever becoming too dry.

The milk is excellent from December to May, because our pastures are located in Macomer at 650 meters above sea level and the sheep always eat fresh grass. Then, the fertilization starts again and there is a physiological decrease in milk production, in addition to the fact that the temperatures rise, the fresh grass is gradually less and less available and the sheep go dry in July. Anyway, our 1,800 sheep are lucky, because they have 200 hectares of pasture at their disposal with more than 100 different types of herbaceous essences.

To be precise, the period of "good milk" can be further divided:

- **Winter,** from December to February: the grass is very lush and the sheep are in good shape at the beginning of lactation, so the milk is fattier and the cheese has a softer and sweeter texture that holds more humidity and lends itself to slowed curing plus the low temperature.

- **Spring,** from March to May: the meadows are covered with flowers, but the milk less fatty, which means that the cheeses tend to dry more quickly and badly withstand long aging even if the pecorino becomes more complex with more or less marked herbaceous notes.
- **Summer,** in June and July: the pasture is rather dry because the milk is now at the end of lactation and the cheeses can no longer be taken into consideration for the "seasoned" version.
- **From August to November** milk is not available.

To end this excursus about milk and the best cheesemaking period, it's important to add that the cheese is periodically greased with a mixture of wine vinegar, olive oil and salt to prevent the formation of molds in the crust.

Finally the name "Fiore" (flower) seems to derive from the use of molds of wild pear wood or chestnut on the bottom of which a flower similar to an asphodel or a peony rose was carved. Others argue that the name came from the fact that historically the rennet originated from the thistle flower. You know the border that divides history from legend is always very difficult to trace, but it helps storytelling and creates curiosity.

OUR CHEESES

Organic Fiore Sardo DOP "dei pastori"

It's important to know that Fiore Sardo made by shepherds is a Presidium Slow Food. It would be a "fermier" product if Sardinia was located in France. We are proud to produce such a symbolic cheese.

The Presidium was founded to safeguard the traditional production of Fiore Sardo in a few small towns in the Barbagia region. Here, a handful of cheesemakers hold and pass on the secrets of artisanal cheesemaking, producing cheese with the whole, raw milk of Sarda sheep, without introduced cultures, with natural rennet that they produce themselves, and with a natural coating. The quantities of traditional Fiore Sardo produced are quite small, but the quality of the cheese is extraordinary – and yet, Shepherds' Fiore Sardo is at risk of extinction. The Presidium producers work to make their cheese known outside the local area to guarantee the survival of an ancient product and practice. At the same time, in the market you can find a basic Fiore Sardo DOP made by bigger companies that use mixed milk coming from different shepherds. Anyway, the DOP regulations oblige producers of the consortium to produce with raw milk, which is quite positive.

Organic pecorino cheese

This is our unpasteurised semi-aged Pecorino. On the crust it presents the pattern of the basket where the curd is drained. For this reason it belongs to the family of "canestrato" (basket) cheeses. The rind is treated with olive oil to avoid cracks. The cheese is aged for a minimum of 4 months in our cellar, and lamb rennet is used whilst the curd is uncooked. The texture presents an ivory white colour. The taste continues to be the backbone of the milk, which is based on the aromatic notes of the Sardinian pastures. The University of Sassari has found more than 50 different essences in 4 square meters of pastures, which include Campeda clover (specific of this area), ryegrass and various flowers.

Ricotta Mustia or Smoked Ricotta Salata

This is a salted ricotta made from the whey coming from the Pecorino production. After a few days of draining, the ricotta is smoked in the same room of Fiore Sardo and then matured for a minimum of 20 days. The term "mustia" comes from the local dialect and it means "smoked". The taste is sweet and intense at the same time, the texture is crumbly and juicy at the same time. Generally it is eaten pure with a few drops of olive oil or grated over "malloreddus", a typical pasta of Sardinia.

SAFEGUARD THE TRIAD

We are lucky to do a job that has existed for thousands of years: we are shepherds first and cheesemakers second. The torch has been passed on to us by our father and, and figuratively speaking, we would do the same with our actual and future colleagues. For sure, our job isn't an easy one, with long days of working, hard conditions and a market that doesn't always recognize the dignity of our products, yet it gives back a lot. It's a job that keeps us connected to the rhythm of nature, to an ancient lifestyle that is made by rusticity, simplic-

ity and craftmanship, but that guarantees dignity and satisfaction. The real cheese world should preserve and safeguard the triad: pastures – animal – raw milk. The farmer takes care of the pastures through turnover and rest. The animal always has fresh sources of grass of little plants and produces and high quality milk expressive of the terroir. The cheesemaker respects the milk working in absence of heat treatment. Can we do better? Yes, we can produce our own ferments to be added to milk, this is the new frontier or even better, the old school which is becoming new again. For us, this is the best way to get real cheese.

TASTE PROFILE

PECORINO
Formaggi Debbene

Italian sheep cheese

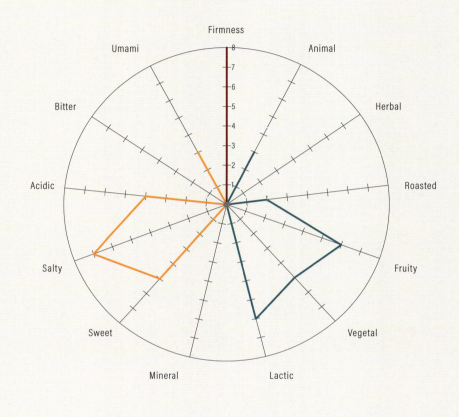

■ texture　　■ aroma　　■ flavour

TEXTURE	**FIRM, STICKY AND GRAINY**
DOMINANT FLAVOURS	**GRASS**
	HAZELNUTS, WALNUTS
	BUTTERMILK, YOGURT
SUBTLE NOTES	**HAY**
	BARNYARD, MEAT BROTH
	HINT OF SMOKINESS
WINE TIPS	**A SPICY RED WINE**
	e.g. the GSM blend (Grenache – Syrah – Mourvèdre)

L'ETIVAZ AOP

an artisan product from an alpine lifestyle

CHEESEMAKERS

L'Etivaz AOP
*Produced by 70 families,
united in a cooperative since 1932
which is responsible for the maturation*
Pays-d'Enhaut, Vaud
SWITZERLAND

WWW.ETIVAZ-AOP.CH

CHEESE IS THE MOST IMPORTANT AGRICULTURAL EXPORT PRODUCT. ALMOST 40% OF THE CHEESE PRODUCED IS SOLD ACROSS THE WORLD.

SWITZERLAND: CENTURY-OLD CHEESE CULTURE

Approximately 80% of Switzerland is covered with natural grasslands, unfavourable for arable farming. Those grasslands enable domestic livestock production and are maintained through grazing of the cattle and harvesting the grass. Without animal farming the grasslands would soon become overgrown. The mountain region would no longer be inhabited and an attractive leisure and recreational space would be lost as a result. The dairy economy contributes to sustainable and decentralised land use.

The Swiss have been making cheese for centuries, for both their own consumption and export. As Swiss farmers have traditionally relied on livestock farming, making cheese was a way to preserve milk which would otherwise spoil rapidly. The first medieval source

mentioning cheesemaking dates back to 1115. Rapidly, cheese grew into an important commercial commodity. A flourishing trade over the Alps to Italy was developed in the 15th century. Cheese was traded for wine and salt or used as a payment method.

In 2020, there were 18,396 milk producers, producing 3,405,139 litres of milk. Decentralised cheesemaking is typical of Switzerland. Dairy farms are a family business and have an average of 25 cows. Almost half of the milk supplied by dairy farmers is turned into cheese. The 203,791 tons of cheese produced in 2020 represent more than 600 different cheeses. Eleven cheeses are protected by the AOP (Apellation d'Origine Protégée) label. Almost two thirds of those cheeses are produced in small cheesemaking facilities by highly trained professionals. Cheesemakers receive fresh milk each morning and evening from their local farmers and process it daily. The short transport distances contribute to an ecological process.

The Swiss dairy industry is one of the most sustainable types of agricultural production. It is of great economic importance that goes far beyond the production of high-quality cheese as it also secures employment and an income for many occupation groups in remote areas. Cheeses from Switzerland are renowned for their quality, their purity, and their good flavour. Animal welfare, production guidelines, controls and environmental regulations are all very strict. To this day, Swiss cheese remains a natural product, with zero tolerance for the use of preservatives, food colourings or flavour enhancers.

The numerous cheese varieties can be subdivided into different categories. Extra-hard cheeses have an especially long ripening period behind them. The most prominent Swiss extra-hard cheese is Sbrinz AOP. There is a wide selection of hard cheeses, a category that includes Emmentaler AOP, Le Gruyère AOP and L'Etivaz AOP. Appenzeller®, Raclette du Valais AOP and Tête de

Moine AOP rank among the semi-hard cheeses. Soft cheeses, on the other hand, ripen relatively quickly. La Tomme Vaudoise and Vacherin Mont-d'Or AOP are renowned Swiss soft cheeses.

Cheese is the most important agricultural export product. Almost 40% of the cheese produced is sold across the world.

L'ETIVAZ AOP: REGION OF ORIGIN

Nestled high in the south-western Alps, L'Etivaz is situated in the district of the Pays-d'Enhaut, one of the 19 old districts of canton de Vaud, in the Vaudois pre-Alps at an altitude of 1,000 metres. The district has 4,600 inhabitants spread over three villages: Château d'Oex, Rougemont and Rossinière.

L'Etivaz is a hamlet of the village of Château d'Oex and has 150 inhabitants. The residents of L'Etivaz have managed to maintain their heritage of traditional cheesemaking and the alpage way of life, which dates back to the 12th century. This small hamlet is the epicentre of the L'Etivaz AOP cheese production and the location of the ripening cellars.

The origin of the word L'Etivaz (the "z" is not pronounced, the "L" is inseparable from the name) comes from the word "l'estivage" which means "migration of herds to mountain pastures where they stay during the summer". Every year, after the snow has melted, 70 cheesemakers and their families will make the journey from the valley and lead their cows up the mountains to join their alpine chalets, a kind of mountain hut or farmhouse, in late spring and summer to produce L'Etivaz AOP. There are 130 chalets, which accommodate the cheesemaking facility, cow sheds, and living quarters. Some of the families own several, at varying altitudes, so they can move their cows when grass becomes scarce. This transhumance, when cattle are taken up to the higher pastures (the alpage) for the summer, is called the "*inalpe*". The cows only graze herbs, grasses, and flowers on the rich, lush Alpine pastures, between 1,000 and 2,000 metres. L'Etivaz AOP cheese will be produced during the official season that lasts from May 10 to October 10.

L'ETIVAZ AOP AND THE HISTORY OF THE COOPERATIVE

The history of L'Etivaz AOP is quite special. Back in 1932, thirty local cheesemakers decided to work collectively to ensure that the ancient style of alpine cheese-making remained alive. That same year they founded their own cheesemakers' cooperative and established their own strict standards. The L'Etivaz brand was born. The idea of the cooperative was to create a centralized facility to ensure a constant cheese quality and to save the independent producers both from the stress of selling the products and the burden of maturing the cheese – a procedure which could not be safeguarded in the alpine chalet because of the poor storage conditions.

The first cellars of the cooperative were built in 1934 with a storage capacity of 3,200 wheels. Cheesemakers brought their freshly produced cheese down from their farms, to be matured and then sold.

The cooperative expanded several times in 1946, 1974, 1986, 2005 and 2012. Today, 30,000 wheels can be stored. 70 cheesemaking families are part of the farmers' collective, which is run by a small team.

The cooperative has a very active role in monitoring the production quality of L'Etivaz AOP. This resulted in obtaining the AOC (Appellation d'Origine Contrôlée) status on 24 September 1999. L'Etivaz became the first food product in Switzerland to be granted the AOC status. Since 2013 the appellation followed the European standards and became AOP (Appellation d'Origine Protégée), following very strict legal specifications ("Cahier de charges L'Etivaz AOP") governing all aspects of milk, feed, production, maturing, etc. An independent and impartial external organisation takes part in the quality control.

NO CHEESE WITHOUT MILK

There is no cheese without milk, and no milk without cows. Usually, the L'Etivaz AOP producers tend herds of Simmental, Holstein, Red Holstein and Brown Swiss cows. Cows contribute to the preservation of the landscape: without their grazing, the alpine grassland would gradually turn into shrubs and, ultimately, to forests.

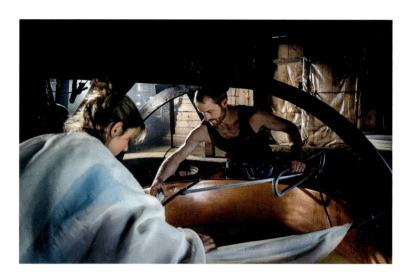

High altitude soils have a poor nutritive quality. The manure of cows releases nutrients, enriching the soil which in turn contributes to a wider botanical variety of herbs, grasses and flowers with their own aromatic compounds. The altitude and this grass-rich diet affect the milk fat composition. The milk contains less saturated fat than the milk of cows grazing in the valley and is rich in omega-3 fatty acids. This results in a slightly smoother texture with a deeper yellow colour of the paste.

All those grasses, herbs and wildflowers transmit their aromas to the milk and create the unique flavour of L'Etivaz AOP. The taste of the cheese may vary as the species-rich pastures differ from one another. This gives a distinct "terroir" to the L'Etivaz AOP.

Other elements positively affecting the quality composition of the milk are the ban of mixing the milk from several herds and the travel restriction from the moment the cows are milked to when the milk is made into cheese. Only a few metres of movement are allowed.

LIFE OF AN ALPINE CHEESEMAKER

Living and working in the chalet is a family affair. Cheesemaking is hard work and can't be done alone. Young and old, all have their own task.

Upon their return from the pastures in the early morning, the cows are milked and afterwards they have a rest in the shed, before going back to the pastures. The morning milk is poured into a huge copper vat. The evening milk will be added after it has been skimmed. When milking the cows in the evening, the cheesemaker stores it in tubs in the milk room, a well-ventilated room located at the northern side and thus the coldest part of the chalet, until the following morning. The temperature should not drop under 18°C. At this temperature, the lactic acid bacteria naturally present in the milk begin to multiply. In the morning, the cheesemaker skims off the cream with a ladle. The cream (a 50 percent fat product called *crème double*) is stored in a handmade wooden pot, called a *diètzè*. It is served with a hand-carved wooden spoon at breakfast or as a dessert with the delicious swiss meringues.

The evening milk needs to be processed within 18 hours. It can never leave the property. The following morning, it will be added to the morning milk. The milk in the copper vat is slowly heated up to 30°C - 32°C, the temperature of the milk when leaving the udder. As the ashes of the fire rise into the chalet's rafters, some might fall into the open vats, which will give the curds a slightly smoky flavour. The cheesemaker will then add special lactic acid bacteria cultures plus the *rennet*, a milk-curdling enzyme produced in the stomach of an unweaned calf. Adding these cultures increase the acidity in the milk, which boosts the effect of the rennet. After stirring the milk for a few minutes, the cheesemaker stops the mixing and allows the milk to rest 35 to 40 minutes so that the curdling coagulation process can start, thickening the milk into a solid ivory pudding-like substance. The trained eye of the cheesemaker observes the consistency of the curd. A lot of cheesemaking relies on instinct and feeling. When the cheesemaker feels the curd has reached the required firmness, he uses the cheese harp to cut the curd into small pieces. This cheese harp consists of a stainless-steel rod with evenly spaced wires.

This operation is crucial and determines the evolution of the cheese. The delicate operation requires a lot of know-how on the part of the cheesemaker. The longer the cheese is stirred with the harp, the smaller the particles of curd and the harder the cheese will be. The finer the curd, the less moisture will be retained and the harder the final cheese will be. This process can take up to an hour and a half.

At this point, the cheesemaker will stir and heat up the curd. After 40 to 50 minutes, a temperature of 57°C will be reached. This warming up is crucial for the development of the taste and the evolution of the cheese. Stirring and warming the curds causes the granules to contract and separate from the whey. The cheese increasingly solidifies. The cheesemaker tests the firmness, and the curd can be removed from the vat.

The cheesemaker stretches a cheesecloth over the suspension arm. With a helper he slides it under the particles and lifts out the cheese mass. The whey escapes from the cloth. He then puts the grains into the *routzes*, perforated moulds that are lined with cloth and that have a diameter of 30 to 45 centimetres. The lid is placed over the cheese and the cheese is compressed. This gives the cheese the desired shape and also helps to drain off excess whey.

The cheesemaker will now place the L'Etivaz AOP casein mark. This numbered label is provided by the cooperative. The cheesemaker adds his accreditation number and the production date, and together they make the "cheese passport". This mark helps to trace the wheel to its origin. It guarantees the authenticity of the cheese, and should problems occur during quality control, the cheesemaker could be identified. The wheels are pressed again until the following morning. Moulds are turned 5 to 7 times during the first 20 hours. The wheels are rubbed with salt and kept at the chalet cellars for 3 to 7 days.

After the cheesemaking of the day, the cowherds build up the cows' feed reserve for the winter. Herbs are cut and stored to feed the cows in winter. The sun and alpine wind will dry them and transform them into hay.

Life in the chalet follows this pace until the end of the season. Then comes the time of the *désalpe*. After spending the summer months in the high alpine pastures making cheese, the farmers, their families and their cows come down from the mountains at the end of September to rejoin their winter quarters. It is a yearly festive event in which the cows are dressed up in their finest floral headdresses and decorative cow bells, called *sonnailles*, and the farmer families dress in traditional outfits to make their way home, down from the mountains to their villages.

During winter, farming continues in the valley. The cattle eat the forage harvested during summer and their milk is sent to the local dairy cooperative.

Besides farming, cheesemakers have often taken part in different activities in the winter, and may work as lumberjacks, woodworkers, mechanics, ski instructors, and other occupations.

DESCRIPTION OF THE CHEESES

There are two types of L'Etivaz AOP: L'Etivaz AOP and L'Etivaz à Rebibes AOP. The word *rebibes* probably originated from the word *rebiffer* or *rebique*. It evokes the shape of the cheese after it has been scraped using a wooden slicer, called the "hobel slicer". Cylinders or rolls are formed. They are served at very special occasions.

Both are made from raw cow's milk exclusively grass-fed from alpine pastures, no silo feed, rennet produced in the stomach of an unweaned calf, and lactic acid bacteria cultures. All ingredients are guaranteed GMO-free.

L'Etivaz AOP

L'Etivaz AOP is made in small quantities: less than 20,000 wheels are produced each year.
Rind: Natural and brownish crust, with morge
Paste: Fairly thin, supple, slightly firm, ivory yellow, the presence of holes is rare
Taste: Frank and aromatic, fruity, light nutty flavour, slight smoky taste
Affinage: In the cellars of L'Etivaz: minimum 5 months

L'Etivaz à Rebibes AOP

Rind: Uniformly yellowish / smear removed, clean, smooth
Paste: Pale yellow, the presence of holes is rare
Taste: Frank and aromatic, fruity, light nutty flavour, slight smoky taste
Affinage: After 6 months of maturing in the L'Etivaz cellars, a selection of L'Etivaz AOP cheeses is made and naturally dried in an attic for a minimum of 30 months

AFFINAGE OF THE WHEELS IN STAGES

Two to three times a week, cheese producers take their wheels to the cellars of the Cooperative at L'Etivaz for the maturing process to start.

The cheese wheels are placed in a brine bath. This highly concentrated salt solution is essential for the rind formation of the cheese, which plays a key role in the preservation and the development of its taste.

At different stages, wheels will rest in distinct cellars at different temperatures and humidity levels, where they are turned over and rubbed with salt. The combination of temperature and humidity level of the cellars boosts the development of micro-organisms giving the rind its orange colour. This is called the smear, or *morge*, and plays a key part in the development of the cheese's aroma. Finally, the wheels are moved to the ripening cellar. They are laid out on un-planed shelves of spruce. They will rest for a period lasting between 5 and 24 months. During this ripening period the L'Etivaz AOP acquires its fine texture and elasticity, and its characteristic yellow ivory colouring.

In addition to the casein mark stamped by the cheesemaker when the cheese is put under the press, the cooperative adds an additional measure: in October 2015 *hot brand marking* was introduced. Every wheel of cheese is branded around the whole of its heel, thus making it possible to authenticate it even when it is cut into segments and therefore protect consumers against fraud.

In October, all L'Etivaz cheesemakers are personally invited to the cooperative. The total weight of the cheeses produced during the season is calculated, while the taxation commission observes the wheels to check their

shape and the colour of the rind. A little hammer knocks and detects eventual abnormalities of the paste, like the formation of holes, which are not allowed. A cheese drill takes a sample of the paste, which then will be tasted to check the flavour. Points are given. In order to become a L'Etivaz AOP the score needs to be at least 15 points out of 20.

The wheels are then classified in premium choice A, B, or C. Second choice is bought by the cooperative and may be sold locally under another name.

In December or January, around 1,000 wheels are selected to undergo a further stage of maturation. The smear is removed from the wheels, which then are oiled. They are stored in an upright position in the attic of the cooperative where they dry out naturally and become the "*rebibes*" version of L'Etivaz after a maturation of a total of 36 months.

TASTE PROFILE | L'ETIVAZ AOP

Swiss hard summer cheese made from cow's milk

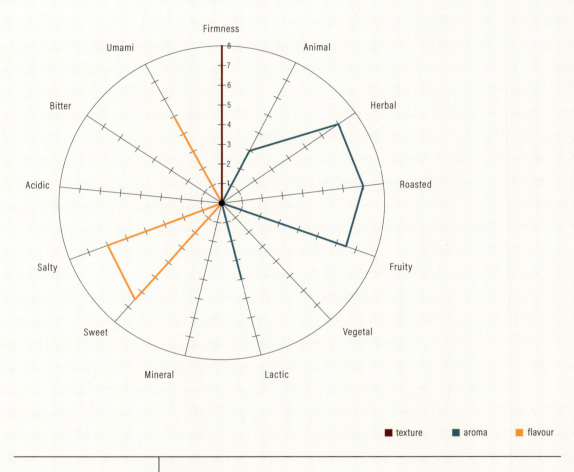

TEXTURE	FIRM
DOMINANT FLAVOURS	**HAZELNUTS**
	CARAMEL
	BEURRE NOISETTE
	SPICES
	HEATHER
SUBTLE NOTES	**BARNYARD**
	COOKED MILK
WINE TIPS	**MORE COMPLEX WHITE WINE WITH SOME BARREL AGING**
	e.g. Chardonnay or a barrel aging Chenin Blanc
	OXIDATIVE WHITE WINE
	e.g. type Vin Jaune (Savagnin) or type Fino Sherry (fortified)
	FULL, SPICY RED WINE
	e.g. Bordeaux blend (Merlot, Cabernet Sauvignon, Cabernet Franc) or GSM blend (Grenache, Syrah, Mourvèdre)

NEAL'S YARD DAIRY

selecting and maturing outstanding British cheese

CHEESE AFFINEUR

JASON HINDS
Neal's Yard Dairy
Founded in 1979
London
UNITED KINGDOM

WWW.NEALSYARDDAIRY.CO.UK

THE FACT THAT NEAL'S YARD DAIRY BEGAN LIFE AS A PRODUCER OF CHEESE, BEFORE EVOLVING INTO A CHEESE SELLER AND MATURER, IS FUNDAMENTAL TO OUR STORY AND PHILOSOPHY.

BRITISH CHEESE CULTURE

Most people, when they think about strong European cheese cultures, think of France, Italy and Switzerland before they think of Britain. Yet the cheese culture in the UK goes back not just centuries, but millennia: there are records of cheese being made to a "crumbly" British-style recipe that date back to Roman times, and up until recently that cheese – known now as Cheshire – was the one most likely to feature on kitchen tables around the country. At the outbreak of World War I in 1914, there were two thousand Cheshire makers in Britain – and that's before you get to cheeses like Cheddar and Wensleydale, of which there were hundreds of small-scale, farmhouse makers.

It is this rich and deep-rooted cheese culture that we lost over the course of the 20th century. During and after World War II, with rationing going on well into the 1950s, there was an overriding need to make food that was cheap and plentiful, and that pushed everything towards mass production. The move towards industrial production of almost all food saw farming and cheesemaking expertise shift from people with a deep technical understanding towards systemised factory cheesemaking: a disappearance aided and exacerbated by the proliferation of supermarkets and the erosion of local grocers, who had previously been some of the greatest champions of regional farmhouse cheeses.

Added to this, the expansion of Britain's railway network into rural areas gave milk producers a market for liquid milk in cities, meaning that farms were no longer obliged to preserve their milk by making cheese. By the end of World War II there were only 45 farmhouse Cheshire makers. By the time you get to 1979, the year Neal's Yard Dairy emerged on the scene, the landscape around us was very bleak indeed.

Back then there were only a handful of farmhouse makers of Cheddar still standing, and they were dwindling fast. Only the Appleby family and a couple of others were still making farmhouse Cheshire, and by the 1990s only the Applebys were left standing. There were a few producers making cheese on a small scale, but it was mostly for their own consumption: there was no large-scale appetite for cheese of that type and quality. The fact that, forty years later, there are now four farmhouse Cheddar makers in Somerset (including two new makers in the last twenty years), as well as Isle of Mull Cheddar in Scotland and Hafod in Wales, is evidence of the renaissance in cheese culture that has taken place in Britain – as is the healthy proliferation of many other native and non-native cheeses.

TRAVELLING CHEESE LOVER

I trace the beginning of my journey into cheese back to my formative years in a French school in Cairo, where the currency of the playground was Asterix and Tintin stickers. It so happens that these stickers could be obtained by the purchase of a box of Laughing Cow cheese. At this point in time – the early 1970s, just after the death of President Nasser – there were very few trappings of the west in Egypt, and only one shop where we could buy European items. We feasted on these French comic books and the cheeses that had the stickers inside. My brother and I would stick them on our suitcases as trophies. And while it's a long way between eating cheese for Asterix stickers and being a partner in Neal's Yard Dairy, the reality is that one's route into quality cheese is unlikely to start with raw milk, farm-made cheese. Because I started my cheese journey at a young age, when we moved back to the UK when I was ten, I was the one who insisted on going to the cheese aisle in Sainsbury's; then, as I got older, to the local delicatessen instead of the supermarket. By the time I got to university, I was really interested in good quality cheese.

It was there that I discovered that we had great British cheese. Up until then, the cheese I had bought was made in France or Italy; but when I discovered Keen's Cheddar and Colston Bassett Stilton, both then made with raw milk – well, that was a hallelujah moment. When it came to the end of university and I started thinking about what I would do for the rest of my life, there were only two things I was truly passionate about, and which would make for a viable career: travelling and cheese. So, I put those two things together and came up with the idea of exporting great British cheese.

A TRADITION OF TASTING CHEESE

The fact that Neal's Yard Dairy began life as a producer of cheese, before evolving into a cheese seller and maturer, is fundamental to our story and philosophy. When the business was started in July 1979, Randolph Hodgson – our founder – was experimenting with making a few fresh cheeses and other dairy products. This journey of discovery inspired him to visit and exchange notes with other likeminded spirits who were making cheese around the country. The questions Randolph and his fellow "new wave" cheesemakers were asking – chiefly, why the same cheese made on the same farm to the same recipe could become so many different versions of itself – led to the establishment of a new network of cheesemakers. Being present in London, it became clear that Randolph had the capacity to sell cheeses beyond his own, and in doing so he could champion the cheeses of the UK's new wave.

Randolph was still keen to understand the variation between one batch and the next, and by buying cheese for the business he had the opportunity to taste cheeses from different batches on a regular basis. This put in motion the act of regularly grading cheeses and selecting those he liked best. That was in the early 1980s, and it proved supremely important in influencing the direction of our business: to this day we make regular trips to cheesemakers to taste different batches, learn more about the variations and grade the cheeses before returning to London. The other Damascene moment was Randolph's realisation that it is one thing to think you have good cheese, and quite another for your customers to agree with you – which is why he decided to offer a taste of the cheeses to all the customers who walked through his shop door.

This created a culture – unique to Neal's Yard Dairy at the time – of really engaging with the customer, talking to them about the cheese, asking them what they like (and don't like) about it. These days the priorities have changed slightly, in the sense that many of our customers are familiar with the cheeses we sell in a way they weren't back then, but what is still unknown to them is the difference between the batches – that the batch we have now is different from the batch we had last week or a month ago. That's why we still need to continuously check in with people to ensure that they are tasting something they like: whether it's with customers in a shop, with producers on a farm or with our colleagues in our London maturing rooms, tasting the cheese – and discussing the cheese we're tasting – is central to everything we do.

It is as fundamental to our work as cheese maturers, or "affineurs:, as it is to our work as cheesemongers. The word affineur comes from the French word "to finish" – which suggests it only applies to the work we do when the cheese is in our possession. Yet while you can do a certain amount of work to influence the quality of

IT IS ONE THING TO THINK YOU HAVE GOOD CHEESE, AND QUITE ANOTHER FOR YOUR CUSTOMERS TO AGREE WITH YOU.

> THOUGH THERE IS PLENTY OF AMAZING CHEESE MADE WITH PASTEURISED MILK, WE REMAIN STRONG ADVOCATES FOR RAW MILK CHEESE.

a cheese during maturation, the roots of good quality always lie in the milk and the make. By visiting the cheesemakers, developing a relationship with them, tasting with them and establishing a constant dialogue, we can influence quality to a greater degree than we ever could through finishing.

As a result, a healthy proportion of the cheese we buy we have already seen by the time it arrives at the maturing rooms. In some cases, our job is simply that of custodian: ensuring that while the cheese is in our care, we treat it the best we can by giving it the right conditions in which to thrive. In other cases, more extreme cases, we create a new cheese, quite different to the one that arrived. Crudely speaking, the job of an affineur is to provide an environment where the cheese is well looked after, having already established it is of a calibre they want to sell to customers. How we achieve that is by having an experienced team of people who are constantly making decisions, because as the same cheese can vary from one week to the next, so the conditions that best suit it might vary too.

There are no hard and fast rules; it's all about making choices in the moment, and the people best qualified to make those choices are the people who work with cheese every day. This work involves a lot of questioning. We have good facilities – different rooms offering different levels of humidity and temperature – but we need people who are constantly alert to the state of each cheese, asking themselves if it is ready for sale, or needs moving to a different room.

That said, it is not just the team turning and moving cheese who are part of the affinage process. The only way we can have a holistic system in which we can continue to learn about the cheese and improve its quality is through feedback – so the retail cheesemongers, customers and producers are all part of it too. If all the parts of the chain are not coherently connected, then the quality will struggle. We need to be on farms, but we also need to have people in the shop talking to customers – and in a sense, that is the most important part. The whole process of cheesemaking is only really completed when the cheese is sold.

Because the chain of production to sale is short, and Neal's Yard Dairy is involved in every element of it, we have the ability to profoundly influence the quality of the cheese. We have all this information about the cheeses and our customers' preferences, and now the team is looking at understanding even more: whether that's moisture content, acidity profiles, rind cultures and so on. We are in it together, in a way that a conventional, industrial cheesemaker with a longer chain could never be.

As a community, the biggest danger we face is any perceived threat to cheese made with raw milk. Though there is plenty of amazing cheese made with pasteurised milk, we remain strong advocates for raw milk cheese. There have been moments in the past – and will probably be moments in the future – when, either through government lobbying or the ramifications of a tuberculosis outbreak, the use of unpasteurised milk will be threatened, so we need to make sure we are working together to extol its virtues.

As a business, I hope we can create an environment that is going to be attractive for people to see a career path for themselves: either as a farmer, maker or someone maturing and selling farmhouse cheese. When I first started working in this industry in the early 1990s, the idea of becoming a cheesemonger or maker was almost risible. Now, thanks to consumers being interested in real cheese and prepared to pay a premium that protects the system that produces it, people are starting to see cheesemaking and selling as a vocation rather than a lifestyle choice. We have a new wave of cheesemakers coming through, which is fantastic – yet the threat faced by small dairy farms producing milk of quality is still very real, because the food system we have in the UK does not reward them for it. As the farmhouse cheese industry expands, there is an opportunity to give added value to these small milk producers by helping them establish and refine partnerships with aspiring cheesemakers. Good-quality milk is, of course, the raw material that underpins everything we do.

TOP 3 CHEESES

My desert island cheese is Colston Bassett Stilton: a gentle, buttery blue cheese with delicate veining. It's the cheese that introduced me to the career path I am in, and the one that made me realise that cheese in Britain can be great. Interestingly, it is neither raw nor farmhouse – but it is traditional, which is a word that gets bandied around a lot these days, often with little justification. Yet tradition is truly maintained at Colston Bassett Dairy because very little changes. Billy Kevan, the head cheesemaker and general manager, is only the fourth cheesemaker they've had since 1913, when the dairy was established. A primary reason their cheese is amazing is because they haven't messed around with it: they have a good team that hasn't changed a lot and is focused on quality.

Of course, the purpose of this book is to focus on and celebrate cheese made on a farm with raw milk – so in the spirit of that I will highlight my two other favourite cheeses: Montgomery's Cheddar and Baron Bigod. Montgomery's Cheddar has been made by the Montgomery family at Manor Farm since 1911 and is one of only three raw milk Cheddars currently being made in Somerset, the birthplace of Cheddar. It is rich, brothy and savoury, with an almost crystalline texture that melts in the mouth. Funnily enough, Montgomery's Cheddar and Colston Bassett Stilton are the two cheeses that get consumed most by volume, not just in my household but in the business as a whole.

That said, there were months in 2021 when we sold more Baron Bigod than we did of either of these cheeses. I like Baron Bigod and its story, because despite not being

made in the Brie region – it's made in Suffolk – it is more authentic than almost any Brie-style cheese currently being produced in France. In terms of how it's made, it ticks more of those traditional Brie de Meaux boxes: it's made on a farm as opposed to a creamery, using the very freshest of raw milk from the farm's herd of Montbéliarde cows, the curds are hand ladled into large moulds using traditional pelle-à-brie ladles, and the young cheeses are salted, wrapped in paper and aged for up to eight weeks in cave-like conditions.

GRAND CRU CHEESES

If we want to keep these traditions, build on them and inspire more people to join the quality cheesemaking revolution, there needs to be an understanding that there is a premium associated with better cheese, just as there is with better wine. At the moment, the cheese industry is not as well organised as the wine industry in helping people to understand this association between price and quality. If you have a burgundy that is many times the price of an entry-level supermarket bottle, people understand that and are happy to pay accordingly. We need people to understand that if they want cheese that is of sublime quality, made on a small scale in a way that means neither the earth's resources nor the people making it are exploited, then that comes with a price.

The word value is another often abused word. People have come to understand that if something is "good value" it is cheap – but that is not true. Value is what you get in return for what you spend. If a cheese is twice the price but tastes four times as delicious, has a richer nutritional content, and has been produced in a sustainable way, then that is much better value – so what we need to do is reassure and encourage people to understand that by investing in a delicious piece of cheese they are investing in a food system that is better for them and the world.

TASTE PROFILE | # MONTGOMERY
Manor Farm

English Cheddar from Somerset made from cow's milk

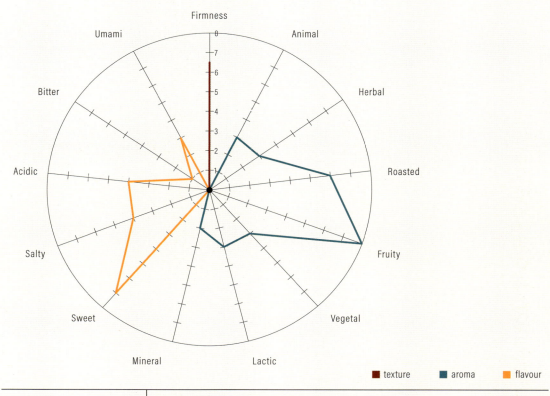

TEXTURE	SEMI-HARD, CRUMBLY AND GRAINED
DOMINANT FLAVOURS	TROPICAL FRUIT (PINEAPPLE) CITRUS NUTS CARAMEL HERBS SMOKED FLAVOUR MEAT BROTH / STEWED MUSHROOMS
SUBTLE NOTES	BEURRE NOISETTE ROASTED ONION FRESH ONION HAY AND STRAW EARTHY TONES
WINE TIPS	**MORE COMPLEX WHITE WINE WITH SOME BARREL AGING** e.g. Roussanne and Viognier with some barrel aging **OLDER COMPLEX RED WINE** e.g. older Nebbiolo or older Pinot Noir

TASTE PROFILE

BARON BIGOD
Fern Farm Dairy

English cow cheese of the Brie de Meaux-type

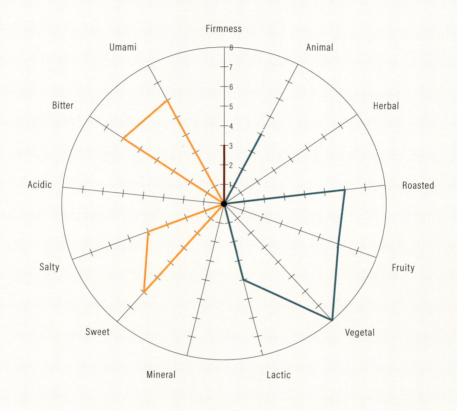

■ texture   ■ aroma   ■ flavour

TEXTURE	**SOFT, STICKY AND RUNNY**
DOMINANT FLAVOURS	**MUSHROOMS, TRUFFLE, EARTHY TONES**
	HAZELNUTS, ROASTED WALNUTS
	CITRUS
	COFFEE
SUBTLE NOTES	**CREAM, BOILED MILK**
	BARNYARD, WET WOOL
	SMOKED DAIRY PRODUCTS
WINE TIPS	**FRUITY RED WINE WITH LITTLE OR SUPPLE TANNINS**
	e.g. Primitovo and Barbera

STICHELTON
the real King
 of
English cheese

CHEESEMAKER

JOE SCHNEIDER
Stichelton Dairy Ltd
Founded in 2006
Cuckney, Nottinghamshire
UNITED KINGDOM

WWW.STICHELTON.CO.UK

THIS QUESTION OF HOW TO TRANSMIT THE KNOWLEDGE AND EXPERIENCE OF ONE GENERATION TO THE NEXT HAS FASCINATED ME EVER SINCE, FOR THIS IS THE ONLY REAL WAY TO PRESERVE THE TRADITIONS AND CRAFTSMANSHIP OF ARTISAN CHEESEMAKING.

BRITISH CHEESE TRADITION

I started my cheese making career as an American living in Holland making Greek cheese for a Turk, and many years later I am making a traditional blue cheese in the heart of England. So if I am asked what the cheese culture is like in my own country, that is a complex question for me to answer. I grew up in New York State, and the cheese we bought and ate in the 1970s and 80s came from a supermarket shelf in individually wrapped slices more akin to whipped oils than cheese. I was well into my twenties before I discovered that real Parmigiano didn't come out of a shiny green can. If there was a burgeoning artisanal cheese culture in America in the 1980s, it was invisible to me. It is certainly much different now. A new generation of American cheesemakers have travelled the world in search of knowledge and inspiration and have brought back what they learned to their farms in Wisconsin, Vermont or elsewhere. Some of the most interesting and delicious farmhouse cheeses in the world are now made in the US. I left those shores many years ago for the time-honoured tradition of pursuing a woman (I have since caught her) all the way to the Netherlands. The cheese culture in Holland was so completely different from what I grew up with, and it afforded me the first glimpse of something I had been missing in my experience of cheese. I am now living in England, in great measure because of what was happening here with cheese twenty years ago.

Great Britain has an ancient and unique history of cheesemaking, but I am not a historian so I will limit my comments to the cheese culture that I found when I first visited here in 1995. The first time I visited the Neals Yard Dairy cheese shop in London in those early days, I was struck by all of the shelves laden with huge objects: beautiful cheeses round and tall with blue-grey rinds and pale centres, of all different shapes and sizes. Seeing whole cheeses like this, in their natural state, was a completely new experience for me. British cheese is shaped this way for historical reasons. Unlike our Continental counterparts that tended to be made and consumed locally, British cheeses spent more time on the roads, in the back of horse-drawn wagons travelling from the farms where they were made to markets in faraway towns and cities, so cheeses had to be robust and hardy, stackable and stable. Imagine trying to drive a wagon full of Brie on a five-day trip from Lancashire to London in July. You see this durable characteristic in most of the traditional territorials like Cheddar, Cheshire and Lancashire, and their immense size and sheer presence as objects make them unique in the cheese world. Another thing that beguiled me about the cheeses at Neals Yard Dairy was the way each one celebrated the tripartite relationship of tradition, place and person. The cheese there wasn't just a type, it was Montgomery's Cheddar, Mrs Kirkham's Lancashire, Appleby's Cheshire, all belonging to a place in history where time, geography and generations entwine. I had not seen this in my time living on the Continent – indeed, in many cases, the cheesemaker might be a closely guarded secret by the affineur or shop owner. This indicated to me something special about the British cheese culture at that time. British farmhouse cheesemaking has suffered a steady decline in the last hundred years for reasons that are well documented in the history books. Certainly the war contributed to this decline, because many family farms making interesting local varieties were forced to start making more commoditised cheese, or to send their milk to a factory making such cheese, to help the war effort. After the war, many of these traditional cheesemakers did not return to their craft, eschewing the hard and often under appreciated work for a steady milk cheque from the newly formed Milk Marketing Board. Post-war technology also brought pasteurisation of cheese milk to the fore, and since the 1950s Britain followed on the coat tails of America's cult of hygiene and sterilisation, which viewed raw milk not as an expression of flavour and connection to the land but as a danger. Raw milk cheeses came very close to extinction in the 1980s with looming UK legislation that threatened a total ban on the use of unpasteurised milk, but these efforts to eradicate hundreds of years of Farmhouse cheesemaking traditions and culture were resisted by a handful of luminaries who fought against the misapprehension and fear informing food safety policy at the time. They have also been battling for years against the general indifference of the market to these culturally important cheeses, celebrating in their shops and market stalls the cheeses and the cheesemakers that embody the craft of transforming pasture into pleasure. This renaissance of British cheese was the culture I walked into and fell in love with in the late 1990s, and making a contribution to this noble endeavour has been my life's work ever since.

WHEN SCIENCE MEETS ART

My cheese-making journey began at a BBQ beside a canal in s'Hertogenbosch in the Netherlands, where I met a Turkish chap who was starting feta production to serve the large Turkish community in the Netherlands. We struck up a conversation and I was interested in what he was doing. I had a degree in Agricultural Engineering that I wasn't using and I needed a job, so I asked if I could come and help him make cheese. My cheese knowledge at this time was limited to eating it, so I bought any book I could find in English to learn about transforming milk into cheese. This brings me to one of the interesting experiences I have had in my attempts to learn the craft of cheesemaking: Where does one get the knowledge? There are certainly many books written about cheesemaking, from the intimidatingly technical to the more practical, but as I discovered when I became more interested in learning from real cheesemakers about their craft, the transmission of knowledge and experience is not always straightforward. I started visiting cheesemakers in Holland, Belgium, France and England, going anywhere that would allow me to come for a few days or a few weeks, trying to convince them that my free, inexperienced labour would be more help than hinderance. I met some very wonderful people along the way who were very gracious with their time. Some of the cheesemakers were guarded with their knowledge, as if they suspected an attempt to try to steal some trade secrets. Others were very open, but in many cases I found that people who had been cheesemakers for many years and had a strong intuitive grasp of their craft found it much harder to articulate exactly what was happening in a technical way. This question of how to transmit the knowledge and experience of one generation to the next has fascinated me ever since, for this is the only real way to preserve the traditions and craftsmanship of artisan cheesemaking. Cheesemaking is a complex mix of good, hard empirical science and a bit of mystical alchemy, and this duality has always intrigued me. The exact science of the mechanics of rennet coagulation or starter propagation are there in the literature for anyone to access and understand. The science of cheesemaking is rich and fun to explore, but there is another side that is more nebulous, more to do with experience and knowledge in a way that is difficult to quantify. The expert cheesemakers I have met are not really using science when they use their nose to tell them if a cheese has ripened well, and though they understand what is happening below the surface of the setting milk, it is through the touch of their hands and by using their other senses that they are able to decide whether to cut the curd now or to wait. That is the craft, the art, and they marry up with science perfectly in artisan cheesemaking.

THE CHEESEMAKER AS SHEPHERD

When I started to intuit this duality in cheesemaking, I found the feta making, with pasteurised milk in a small factory, a bit one dimensional. I was attracted to those dark, humid caves I had visited in France, to the deeply satisfying mould growth on cheddar rinds I had seen growing in Somerset. I thought I knew the science part (turns out I didn't), and what I wanted more of was some of that magical alchemy. In the late 1990s, the UK was undergoing a renaissance of farmhouse cheesemaking, cheese selling and general cheese appreciation, so my

STILTON IS DIMINISHED BECAUSE IT IS PROTECTED BY EUROPEAN LEGISLATION, THE RULES OF WHICH STIPULATE THAT ONLY PASTEURISED MILK CAN BE USED. THIS IS A CORRUPTION OF THE PURPOSE OF THE PDO SCHEME, WHICH SHOULD OSTENSIBLY IDENTIFY AND PROTECT REGIONALLY PRODUCED TRADITIONAL FOODS.

gaze turned next to England to pursue a career in cheesemaking. I was invited to join a small Biodynamic farm in Sussex, where I would meet two people who had a profound effect on my philosophy of food and farming. Old Plawhatch Farm was run by Michael and Jayne Duveen, and they used raw milk from the farm's herd of Meuse-Rhine-Ijssel cattle to make cheese, yoghurt and cream. I learned about the vital connection of the land to the food that it produces, how terroir is transmitted from soil to grass, to the cow, to the udder, to the vat. The cheesemaker's role is one of shepherd, taking one of nature's most perfect foods and distilling it down to its most subtle essences without damaging its connection to the land, climate, meadows, animals or people from whence it comes. Even in those early days I aspired to make a cheese worthy of a place on the shelves of Neal's Yard Dairy with all those other great British Farmhouse territorials. In 2000, I started my second project in the UK with the Bamford family on their estate in the Cotswolds. They had a dairy farm, and Lady Bamford wanted to start using the milk for cheesemaking and to create The Daylesford Organic Farmshop for making and selling artisan food. I spent five wonderful years there, honing my craft, working beside impassioned bakers, chefs, farmers and growers who inspired me with their dedication to perfection. Without that experience, I doubt I would have had the confidence or the ability to set out on a journey in 2006 that started over a pint of beer in a pub in Borough Market in London, where Randolph plied me with drink and planted the idea in my head of resurrecting an extinct cheese. It is with the unique story of the extinction of traditional raw milk Stilton in England that my passion for raw milk cheese found perfect focus in the creation of Stichelton.

THE NEW KING OF ENGLISH CHEESE

Stilton has ostensibly been called the King of English cheese, and the story of what happened to Stilton is inextricably bound to the story of why Stichelton exists. To any young cheesemaker I meet, I dispense an unsolicited bit of wisdom. There is a fork in the road for any kind of food production, including cheese. You can go down the route of industrialised production, where ingredients are just inputs, and quality and flavour take a back seat to efficiency. Or you can produce food artisanally, with

your hands, with care for and attention to your ingredients, with only the goal of flavour and the pleasure of eating in mind. Many young people don't even know that the fork in the road exists, so I feel I've done my job in just pointing it out, restraining my evangelism and stopping short of telling them the direction they should take. But I am a cheese evangelist. If I look outside my window right now, I can see the grass in the fields that the cows are grazing, I can see the cloudy weather that hovers over the hill, and the cows eating and ruminating. What was grass yesterday is now part of the milk in the vat below my office, and this morning I walked over to the parlour and chatted with Graham, who milks the cows, decides what they will eat and how much, and chooses what grasses he wants to plant for them. He loves cows and he is in a good mood this morning despite the freezing weather, so I think the milk will be good today. All of these connections go into the flora of the milk: the climate, soil, grass, the barns and the men who tend these animals and milk them all contribute to the character and potential of that milk to be deliciously transformed into cheese, an emblematic ambassador of place. If you pasteurise that milk, kill everything good in it with heat, then you cut all of those connections. You are no longer tied to the land and you are working with an indifferent substrate of fat and protein that could have come from anywhere. Such milk is wholly uninteresting to me. Using your own raw milk to make cheese is essential, but in the late 1980s, the very last raw milk Stilton was made and then became extinct. This is not hyperbole, so I will repeat that traditional raw milk Stilton made on a farm with raw milk is extinct. Randolph Hodgson saw this situation as an egregious affront to the rich history and tradition of British cheese, and, in 2004, sought to address this travesty.

Stichelton is not a Stilton. All Stilton is made with pasteurised milk, and may contain cranberries, nuts, or even a banana if you like, but it cannot be made on a farm with raw milk. Stichelton is made only with our own raw milk and does not harbour fruit or nuts of any kind. Stilton is diminished because it is protected by European legislation called a PDO (Protection of Designation of Origin), the rules of which stipulate that only pasteurised milk can be used. This is a corruption of the purpose of the PDO scheme, which should ostensibly identify and protect regionally produced traditional foods. In the case of the Stilton PDO, instead of protecting small producers and demonstrating adherence to authentic and traditional methods of production, the current PDO affords market protection to a small cartel of very large Stilton producers. The PDO is not inclusive of a community of traditional cheesemakers, it is an intentional barrier to entry for small producers so that the market share can be controlled by a handful of large companies. This raises the question to whom does a PDO belong? If a nation or community has a long tradition of producing a cheese in their region, who owns this tradition? Should our food culture be owned by all of us or by corporations? These corporations may not even have existed when these traditions started, but now they control all aspects of their production. If you understand the importance of this question then you are in our tribe.

SLOW CHEESE

The corruption of the PDO system is a major barrier for any small producers wishing to make a farmhouse Stilton because they will not be able to sell the cheese under the Stilton name unless they pasteurise the milk. Despite these impediments, we decided to persevere with our project to explore the traditional methods of producing this historic British cheese on a farm with raw milk. When we began, we had a rough idea of the type of recipe we wanted to follow – after all, we weren't reinventing the wheel – but the knowledge and experience of making this type of cheese using raw milk was long gone by the time we started, so it has taken years of trial and error to learn how best to make Stichelton. The primary difficulty in making our cheese is that the recipe is very sensitive to initial conditions. Stichelton is unlike most other British territorials in that it is a long, slow make over 24 hours with an acidity development curve of a snail's pace. This long, slow acidity development is what gives the milk the time it needs to fully express its flavour potential, but it also leaves the cheese vulnerable to all sorts of problems along the way. Other recipes afford much more opportunity to influence the make through stirring, heating, curd manipulation and so on, and are made in much shorter periods of time so changes can take place along the way if the acidity or drainage is too fast or too slow. Stichelton is uniquely challenging in this regard and great care is needed in setting up the initial conditions because once the curd is cut there is very little the cheesemaker can do to control these factors. He has far fewer tools in the toolbox to use than makers of other types of cheese, fewer buttons and levers as it were. I like to use the analogy of the sport of curling, where the aim is to get the stone to land in a small circle many meters away down the length of the ice. The curler must set up the exact speed and direction needed to get the stone to stop exactly where he wants it to, but once the stone is released there is nothing left to be done (we are ignoring the hilarious sweeping efforts to bolster our example). This is much like Stichelton making: we must set up the exact homeopathic amount of starter, get the temperature of the milk to its optimum, add just the right amount of rennet and wait for the curd to be perfectly set for cutting, but after this point there is little else we can do and all that remains is to go home for a good night's sleep and come the next morning to see if everything has turned out well, to see where our stone has landed. We don't go through all of this agony for nothing. It is essential to allow a long, slow development of acidity, coupled with a gentle but unhindered drainage of the curd, in order to get the most flavour out of our milk. Add too much starter and you mask the natural organisms in our milk. Squeeze out too much moisture too quickly and you have a drier, harder cheese tasting mostly of starter. Add too little and you get a wet, weak cheese that will collapse on the shelves before it has time to develop deep flavour. Such sensitivity to tiny changes in the recipe requires an empathy with the changes occurring almost weekly in the milk. We have to work closely with the herd manager to stay on top of these seasonal fluctuations in the milk. All factors – what the cows are eating, the season of the year, their stage in lactation – change the behaviour of the milk and add to the complexity of making Stichelton. At the end of the day we are bacteria farmers, and every season offers up a different harvest of flora in the milk that we must anticipate and respond to in our day-to-day decisions. Cheeses made in late summer and autumn, when the fat content of the milk is high because the cows are on good, fresh grass with stable dry matter contents, will be faster ripening, sweeter, full of soft syrupy nectar. Winter cheeses will be tighter, drier, longer to break down and hence more lactic, savoury, meaty. Supermarkets would call this variability inconsistent, but I enjoy the different personalities of Stichelton as the seasons change because it expresses the natural rhythm of the farm throughout the year.

A COMMUNION OF LAND AND TIME

The other cheesemakers and cheesemongers who I love working with care deeply about this expression of their milk. Being connected in this way to people who understand the vital importance of preserving our cultural heritage in food and farming makes me feel that what we are attempting to do is worthwhile. Everywhere in the cheese world I encounter little acts of care and dedication that inspire me. I have a cheesemaking friend whose grandmother would scold him as a lad if he splashed any milk whilst tipping the churn into the vat because he was damaging the milk. Another friend only makes his cheese whilst his cows are out on pasture because he believes the best cheese must come from cows fed on fresh grass. A third generation cheddar maker I know has a store room that is like a cathedral of cheddar. He has big farmer's hands that would be just as comfortable around a welder as a cheese iron. He knows his farm and land intimately, understands the vitality of his cows and the quality of their milk which now lives in the piece of cheese he is holding for us to taste and smell as we stand together. You cannot help but be moved by the beauty of the connections this simple act embodies. It is a communion of land and time transformed and shared with us. A profoundly human gift. Hundreds of cheese shops around the world are inspired by such beauty too. Everyone we sell our cheese to gets it. They are ambassadors who value the integrity that goes into a special cheese that is made by impassioned people from the fruits of their own land, and their mission is simply one of sharing this with others.

FROM CHEESE TO CHURCH

I've used the word craft quite a bit above. Cheesemaking is a craft, made by craftspeople. It takes dedication, skill, a willingness to learn, and perseverance. Have you ever visited an ancient church and gazed at the stones or intricate woodwork that some craftsman put there hundreds of years ago? If I do my job right, if I make delicious authentic cheese that is honest and carries the integrity of the traditions of real cheesemaking at its heart, if it brings pleasure to people so they spend their lives seeking out real cheese and teaching their children about good food, then in hundreds of years after I am gone, people will still be able to eat raw milk farmhouse cheeses and that will be the church I helped to build.

TASTE PROFILE

STICHELTON
Stichelton Dairy

English blue veined cheese similar to blue Stilton but made from raw cow's milk

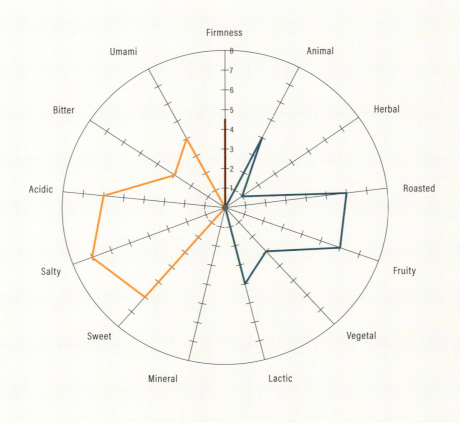

TEXTURE	**SOFT AND BUTTERY**
DOMINANT FLAVOURS	**WALNUTS**
	GRAPEFRUIT
	TOAST, BRIOCHE, BISCUITS
	CARAMEL
	MEAT BROTH
	SMOKED DAIRY PRODUCTS
	BUTTER
SUBTLE NOTES	**MOULD, HUMUS**
	EARTHY TONES
	GREEN APPLE
	WET WOOL
WINE TIPS	**FORTIFIED RED WINE (*VIN DOUX NATUREL*)**
	e.g. type Porto or Banyuls

BWLCHWERNEN FAWR

the longest standing registered organic dairy farm in Wales

CHEESEMAKER

PATRICK HOLDEN
Holden Farm Dairy, Bwlchwernen Fawr
Founded in 1973
Lampeter, Ceredigion, Wales
UNITED KINGDOM

WWW.HOLDENFARMDAIRY.CO.UK

FARMING AS STEWARDSHIP

I enjoy the remarkable privilege of having farmed the same piece of land, around 300 acres straddling a hill in West Wales, continuously for around 50 years. I have always felt that at a higher level land management is really about stewardship. By an accident of fate I've become responsible for nurturing the natural and human capital on a particular farm and at the same time hopefully producing a sustainable surplus of food without depleting the soil or the wildlife, which can coexist with a sustainable farming system, or contaminating the water or the air, upon which elements all farmers depend for a living and should pollute at their peril.

In a way, it would not be an exaggeration to say that the future of civilisation as we know it depends on the capacity of all farmers to undertake this stewardship role – maintaining its natural resources whilst at the same time producing as much as possible with the maintenance of the balance sheet of nature.

On our exposed hill, with lots of rain, fragile soils and an elevation which is not a mountain but nevertheless at 240 metres more challenging than farms at lower levels, the management system which can best be used to achieve these aims is more restricted than the fertile fields at least of England. Put simply, we are a predominantly grassland farm, 50% of which is not really suitable for ploughing at all and therefore is permanent grass. Not just grass, of course, but grasses, clovers and all the other wild plants which can coexist with a sustainable farming system. Even the land which is capable of growing crops for human consumption, perhaps 150 acres at most, can only do so for a couple of years before it needs to enter the restorative and healing process, in our case consisting of herbal lays, a mixture of grasses, clovers, other legumes and herbs including chicory, Yarrow, plantain, sheep's parsley, Burnet plus, of course, the unsown species, including dandelions and a multitude of other welcome weeds.

If you do the maths, that means that in any one year we have around 90% of the farm growing grass, permanent or temporary, with only 10% of the land available to produce food that humans could eat. However, in our case, we have elected to be dairy farmers, and although there are a growing number of farmers who do not feed any grains whatsoever to their cows, we believe this can put a strain on the systems, particular for the young animals, so we use the arable part of our rotation to grow a mixture of oats and peas, which we mill daily and feed to the cows in the parlour.

THE MERITS OF THE DAIRY COW

We've described the key elements of our farming system for a reason: the restricted capacity of the land that we are farming, due to climatic, soil and topographical restrictions, is very typical of much UK farmland in the more marginal areas. Perhaps up to 20% or even more of Britain needs to be farmed in a similar fashion. We are a nation of grass, which of course gives rise to the question: How can we best turn that grassland into food that can nourish and sustain our citizens?

This brings me to promote the merits of the dairy cow in general and in particular of the remarkable capacity of cheese to be part of a sustainable diet. The dairy cow is probably the most efficient way to convert grasses, clovers and other companion plants into food that we can eat – more efficient than beef or lamb. Not only that, for at the end of her generous service as a dairy cow she can also be eaten, as can her calves, unless they are kept as dairy replacements.

All this seems more relevant and important as we move towards a post-industrial chapter of UK agriculture, hopefully harnessing the power of sustainable farming not only to reduce agricultural emissions but perhaps even to be a net carbon sink, drawing down CO^2 from the atmosphere and re-sequestering it in the soil. The dairy farming system I have described above is eminently capable of achieving such results, but only if it is tuned to deliver these much-needed outcomes: high quality nutrient-dense food and an annual contribution to replenish nature's depleted bank of natural capital, particularly the soil. Although my own observation and sporadic data capture has persuaded me that our farming system is already achieving these objectives, my lack of discipline in keeping consistent and accurate records of the impacts of my farming practices unfortunately leaves me unable to back up these assertions with solid data as evidence.

All of the above is a preamble to my homage to cheese. As I now see it the farmer's role, which is a fusion of art, science and alchemy, is to oversee and manage the systemic combination of ecosystems, microbiomes, cycles and relationships – a kind of dance with nature from which one is not separate and if one gets it right can result not only in an ecosystem which is more than the sum of its parts, but also the enormously satisfying outcome of a true surplus of delicious food, a net gain without any trade-offs and damage to the ecosystem as a whole. In this way, if the farm is the macrocosm, the production of cheese is the microcosm, a lens through which one can understand all the laws and principles which inform the system as a whole.

CHEESE CONVERSATIONS

I didn't have a farming background, but formative childhood experiences in nature (in wild places and on farms) coupled with an awakening understanding of the ecological crisis in my late teens had filled me with a desire to go back to the land and create a self-sufficient cultural and agricultural community on a hill in West Wales. The farm has had several chapters, but since I took full ownership in 2003, the business plan has been to improve the infrastructure, add value to the milk and create a cultural and educational centre of learning on the farm. The early years on the farm in the 1970s and 1980s included vegetable production and cereal growing for milling. We soon realised that the only way to derive a secure income with any control was by marketing our produce directly. However, our milk had nearly always been sold anonymously, first through the milk marketing board and then through organic cooperatives.

We realised the second phase of adding value to the milk after a farm visit by members of the Specialist Cheesemakers Association where we took the group on a long farm walk to discuss the implications of farming practice on milk and cheese. This sparked a conversation with my son and daughter-in-law, Sam and Rachel Holden, on how to take cheesemaking on our farm forward. They were lucky enough to learn about cheesemaking through a series of visits to inspirational cheesemakers like Joe Schneider of Stichelton and Simon Jones of Lincolnshire Poacher. Simon was a huge influence, and there is a pleasing circularity in his role in Hafod's beginnings in that he trained with Dougal Campbell, a good friend and a pioneer in the renaissance of British farmhouse cheese who used our farm's milk in the 1980s to make several artisan Welsh cheeses. Simon brought a lot of the elements of his make, which had been informed by his time with Dougal, back to Wales by mentoring and helping Sam and Rachel make their first batch of Hafod in 2007. The technical and emotional support within the farmhouse cheese community was crucial in those early days and reflects a rare but so valuable interconnectedness in a food system, which other areas of food production like horticulture and meat would benefit from.

A METHOD OF TRUSTING

The Hafod recipe has evolved in the last ten years with the discovery of older texts on commercial cheesemaking, notably *Practical Cheddar Cheesemaking* by Dora Saker, and a curiosity within the team to understand the early methods used at farmhouse scale before the "industrialisation" of cheddar production. Our traditional mixed family farming practice using a grass based, low input, organically managed native breed of cow results in a delicious raw ingredient: our milk, which we want to transform into cheese in a slower, more responsive and sensitive way, one that will better reflect the terroir and our farming practice and which will be informed by the milk's qualities of expression.

This spirit of enquiry and an intuitive observation of the universal principles, which guide processes and outcomes, is very much a part of our experience in farming and is an approach that serves us well when processing our milk too. Sam and Rachel have now moved on to a new project, but we continue to be blessed with sensitive cheesemakers with a huge respect for their raw ingredient. At the moment, all of our cheesemakers are also herds persons, as comfortable in the milking parlour or caring for calves as they are in the make room or maturation store caring for the cheese. This interconnectedness is so valuable but only possible because of our farm's smaller size and scale, and it brings a trust and respect to every part of the process.

Trust is at the heart of our farming and cheesemaking. Our landscape-tuned approach to the stewardship of this hill is one based on a deep understanding and confidence that nature can provide, that our role within the ecosystem will be one of nurture and that the outcome will be positive health in the soil, plant and animal. We can therefore trust the milk to be everything that we need it to be and that our intervention in the make room and maturation store need only be one of enabling the transformation of milk to cheese rather than over controlling or dominating that process.

THE BIGGEST CHALLENGE TO THE ART OF CHEESEMAKING IS THE STIFLING BURDEN OF "ENVIRONMENTAL HEALTH" REGULATIONS. WE ABSOLUTELY TRUST THE HEALTH OF OUR ENVIRONMENT AND YET, THERE IS A WIDESPREAD AND MISUNDERSTOOD FEAR OF GERMS.

We remain humble and in wonder of our milk and the cows that produce it and are mindful that we should continually question the impact of our intervention in that transformation. In particular, just as circular economy principles inform our farming, we aim to reduce the external inputs used in the cheesemake. Although cloth binding, for example, is seen as traditional in farmhouse cheddar production, it was, in fact, an early nineteenth century "innovation". We have stopped cloth binding our Hafods and find that our comparatively small (in cheddar terms) 10 kilograms truckles mature more happily, with an ability to self-regulate more effectively without that layer of cloth in our store's environment. Equally, we are working towards replacing commercial starter cultures, which we bulk up in our own milk but that narrow diversity and complexity in farmhouse cheese, by developing our own starter cultures from our milk. We are not unique in this, but it will be an interesting challenge to embrace a more farm-tuned flavour bandwidth in a cheddar using our own farm micro biome as the inoculant for our cheesemaking. In 2017 we made a single experimental batch of Hafod with no starter cultures; we just trusted and allowed the milk's natural microbiology to direct its journey – an incredible learning experience on the true "terroir" of our cheese.

The trust continues in the maturation store where the farming year is represented in cheese and each batch continues to reveal those subtle interactions, relationships and intimate cycles and circles of the hill's thriving ecosystem. The same independent but interdependent microbiological communities inhabit and influence the cheese through maturation as they do in the soil, the plant and the cow's udder, and that balance of nature is respectfully attended and nurtured as we turn, rub and observe the aging Hafods. Our store has a church-like atmosphere and a unique smell that reflects the life in the fields, barns and milking parlour. We are always delighted when our customers talk about the direct connection with the farm that they smell and taste in Hafod on the counter, whether in Wales, Europe or Australia, and whether it is a connection through memory because they have visited or through understanding because they know and relate to our story of place.

RENAISSANCE OF FARMHOUSE CHEESE

It is that understanding for which we are so grateful to our storytellers and champions: the cheesemongers, independent retailers and restaurateurs who are so passionate about understanding the provenance and community behind the cheese that they sell. The renaissance of British Farmhouse cheese and the positive energy and demand that is now allowing small family farms on marginal land like ours to add value and make a living again through more joined up supply chains is due entirely to this passion and enthusiasm. I can confidently say that we have a direct relationship with every customer we sell to and that we are not just a name in a catalogue for any of them: the majority have visited and spent time on the farm and the cheese dairy and have personally experienced that ecosystem and community that they smell, taste and feel in Hafod. It is a privilege for us to be a part of this farmhouse cheese community, and we feel respect, love and admiration for all those working within it.

Within the energy and excitement of this next chapter in British raw milk cheeses, I do feel, however, that the biggest challenge to the beautiful and complex art of cheesemaking and the creativity of capturing and transforming the essence of our land is the stifling burden of "environmental health" regulations. We absolutely trust the health of our environment and yet the widespread and misunderstood fear of germs and the extreme "precautionary principle" adopted by regulators forces small producers to wage war on the very microbiome that is key to our healthy environment and that I, for one, want to celebrate. It has sent some of the most traditional small producers in other parts of Europe underground as they realise that their cheesemaking will no longer tick the boxes. And, as they drop from our awareness, their skill, knowledge and understanding that has been passed on through generations is lost. New entrants to cheesemaking are immediately smothered by the regulations, preventing them from truly exploring what it means to transform milk to cheese because of the bureaucracy, paying the price of proving that they have "food safe" premises and testing regimes, not to mention the expected reliance on costly chemicals with their own environmental impact upstream at manufacture and downstream at disposal.

This stranglehold extends beyond the farm gate to our customers, who, if they are small and independent retailers without whole quality control departments to deliver compliance, are also vulnerable to the "hygiene police".

We are not saying that food quality systems and procedures are not important and of course cleanliness, good housekeeping, care and attention are central to any well run dairy, whether on the slopes of a mountain in the Alps or on a wet Welsh hill. But if through chemical blitzing of environments with the aim of total sterility and the annihilation of all bugs, including the good ones, we win the "war on germs" we'll end up on the losing side, and I fear that this is the current direction of travel.

I am an optimist, though, and have great hopes because one of the key outcomes of sustainable and regenerative farming and food production is the positive health that creates the energy required to navigate through these challenges. I see the science of the microbiome catching up with the intuitive understanding that bacteria are key to our survival. This – along with a recognition of the wealth of almost lost skills and wisdom of artisan makers and the need to restore, maintain and celebrate them before they disappear – brings much to feel excited about.

It is also clear that, given the opportunity, people want to do the right thing: a reevaluation of what really matters is driving change. I see wonderful examples of new farmers, growers and food producers springing up everywhere. A new generation is seeking those same connections with the land that I and my fellow communards searched out in the early seventies. We receive many requests from twenty-somethings from across the world who may have come across us initially through our cheese and want to experience and learn through practice as volunteers on our farm and in the dairy. Our small-scale and joined-up farming and cheesemaking means that as long as they are happy to roll their sleeves up and get "stuck in", their time with us will be intense but productive and wide reaching. Often, their curiosity and spirit energises our community and the learning and influences work both ways.

FUTURE PLANS

For the next chapter for the farm, we hope to become a stage where more gatherings can take place and be inspired by the magic of this hill and what happens here. We hope to host retreats, workshops, educational visits and courses – something that we have always tried to do informally but that we now hope can be extended through improved facilities. We welcomed the Specialist Cheesemakers Association here for their annual

> A NEW GENERATION IS SEEKING THOSE SAME CONNECTIONS WITH THE LAND THAT I AND MY FELLOW COMMUNARDS SEARCHED OUT IN THE EARLY SEVENTIES.

farm visit weekend in 2021 – again, there was a pleasing circularity in seeing that wonderful community all here on the farm and being reminded of the SCA farm walk that we hosted in 2005 that initiated the development of cheesemaking and Hafod on this farm. We were also able to see the James Aldridge Memorial Trophy for Best Raw Milk Cheese, which we won in 2019, passed onto another new cheesemaker from North Wales.

Inspiration from nature and wonder are at the heart of what brought us here in 1973 and have informed each chapter and the farm's evolution since. Hafod is one of the many manifestations of that wonder, which we are reminded of through every sense of the interconnectedness of all living things and of the vitality of the soil, plant and animal life of this hill.

TASTE PROFILE

HAFOD WELSH CHEDDAR
Holden Farm Dairy

Cheddar made from Ayrshire cow's milk

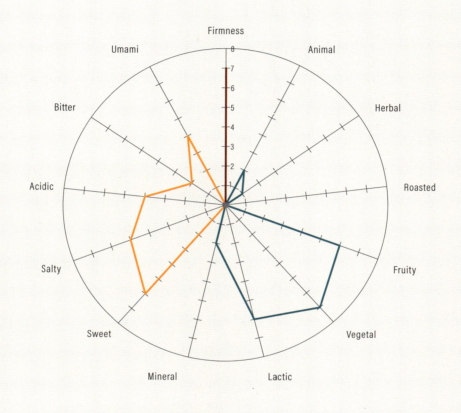

■ texture   ■ aroma   ■ flavour

TEXTURE	**FIRM AND GRAINED**
DOMINANT FLAVOURS	**EARTHY TONES, HUMUS**
	HAY, STRAW
	YOGURT, SOUR CREAM, BUTTER
	NUTS
	GRAPEFRUIT, CITRUS
SUBTLE NOTES	**WET WOOL**
	FLINT
	GRASS
	ONION
WINE TIPS	**FRESH WHITE WINE WITH CRACKLING ACIDS**
	e.g. Albarino, Grüner Veltliner, Garganega
	WHITE PET'NAT (*PÉTILLANT NATUREL*)
	e.g. Sylvaner, Pinot Blanc, Garganega

HOLDEN FARM DAIRY

APPLEBY'S DAIRY
award-winning Cheshire since 1952

CHEESEMAKER

SARAH APPLEBY
Appleby's Dairy
Founded in 1952
Shrewsbury, Shropshire
UNITED KINGDOM

WWW.APPLEBYSDAIRY.COM

TO LANCE AND LUCY, WHO WALKED A SMALL HERD OF COWS FROM WYCHES TO WHITCHURCH IN THE LATE 1940S, CHESHIRE CHEESE-MAKING WAS VERY MUCH PART OF THE LARGER TAPESTRY OF A MIXED DAIRY FARM.

A LINE OF CHEESEMAKING MATRIARCHS

Appleby's has a long history of Cheshire cheesemaking. The dairy was founded by Lance and Lucy Appleby at Hawkstone Abbey Farm in the early 1950s, but Lucy learnt her skill from her mother and most likely from her grandmother too. The matriarchal structure within cheesemaking has been well documented, and Appleby's was one of many dairy farms where the wives and daughters played an enormously significant role in the economics of the business. Lucy not only made cheese and reared seven children, she also sold the farm's produce, kept an incredibly detailed ledger of any business transactions and later in life became an unassuming ambassador of traditional Cheshire cheese.

To Lance and Lucy, who walked a small herd of cows from Wyches to Whitchurch in the late 1940s, Cheshire cheesemaking as an element of the business was a given, the value of it was of huge importance and very much part of the larger tapestry of a mixed dairy farm. The stables for the work horses were converted into a dairy. The same dairy we use today. We are one of very few remaining farmhouse cheesemakers where the cheesemaking still takes place within the farmhouse. Lucy had a connecting door from the kitchen to the dairy where she would wheel the pram. The Cheshire she made fitted into the rhythms of family life, but she was hugely committed to the vat. Touchingly, the notes in the margins of the 1953 make books detail the minutiae of this family life – the date her daughter Ruth first walked, a 21st birthday and so on, as well as the amount of starter culture added, the ripening time and an always critical comment on the final curd. These old books have been invaluable over the years. Only just recently we turned to them when we were struggling to manage the changes that autumn milk has made to the process.

Lance and Lucy were steadfast in their belief in the Cheshire they made, and, as the third generation, we are incredibly grateful for their tenacity. The road they travelled was often rocky, especially as, post war, the face of agriculture rapidly altered. As with almost all types of farming at that time, the focus turned away from slow food production to a fast and aggressive culture where yield became king and farmers were encouraged to chase output. Although the farm's herd grew in those years and liquid milk sales became an ever more important part of the business, almost miraculously cheese production in the converted stable continued – cheese production that stayed true to the area's Cheshire cheese heritage, an uncompromising approach that was increasingly unfashionable. I have gained ever growing respect, as we navigate our own struggles, of the almost sheer bloody-mindedness of Lance and Lucy during this period. From being one of a community of Cheshire makers over 100 strong in the '70s to the startling fact they were a diminishing number must have felt bewildering. But from the ashes of the many British

Territorial cheeses there smouldered a belief by a small minority that the cheese they produced was of value and significance, that it couldn't and shouldn't be entirely compromised and altered by the growth of large-scale cheese factories or an industrial approach to a cheese so rooted in its provenance and territory.

The last straw came in the shape of the Milk Marketing Board in the 1980s who, although in many ways had a positive impact as a farmer-led co-operative in the liquid sales market, were encouraging cheesemakers to produce a Cheshire that was uniform. This uniformity, and the waxing and grading of Cheshire had Lucy and particularly Lance raging at the demands their beloved cheese had thrust upon it. Neither could bear to use wax – it was just too much of a juxtaposition between that of the beautifully handmade cloth-bound cylindrical columns that allowed the cheese to breathe and mature, and the waxed versions that then stayed enshrined ensuring the most value was retained in the form of weight but compromised the essence of Cheshire, the soft giving crumble and the flavour. A flavour and quality that Lance and Lucy prided themselves in.

As the market for Cheshire cheese altered, Lance and Lucy responded by building relationships that became friendships with a handful of men and women for whom these small producers and their cheeses held enormous cultural value. They were instrumental in founding the Specialist Cheesemakers Association, what was then a small group of artisan cheesemakers who came together to highlight a diminishing craft, offer support to each other and encourage more people to make and monger cheese. Randolph Hodgson, one of the founders of iconic cheesemongers Neal's Yard Dairy, was such a huge fan of Lucy he named his puppy after her. The relationship blossomed between Randolph, a bright, articulate Londoner, and Lance and Lucy, farmers and cheesemakers from Whitchurch. There became much more of an urgency and desire to retain these beautiful Territorial cheeses. The handful of mongers dotted around the country had the same passion as the handful of remaining cheesemakers who began to unite, all working to create a healthy market for the likes of traditional raw milk Cheshire, Lancashire and Cheddar.

Lucy taught her craft to a number of people who joined her in the dairy, but Gary Gray, a young 27-year-old out of the forces became her hands as the physicality of Cheshire making became too much. She shared with him her love of cheesemaking, and he rewarded her with a loyalty and commitment to produce a Cheshire cheese that had all the signature traits she was taught by her mother. Lance and Lucy were joined by two of their sons and the business continued to wind its way into the future with forks in the road. Sadly, one son passed away and the remaining son became more focused on liquid milk sales. This response to both the economics of the business and social pressure to become bigger in terms of input and output was seen to be desirable. The traditional mixed dairy farm with lower inputs, less risk and eggs in many baskets was in danger of becoming far more monoculture. The cow numbers were growing and they were permanently housed. The milk from these animals who were fed a consistent diet come winter or summer was far less diverse, far less nuanced and made a Cheshire that was also far less diverse and nuanced.

BACK TO BASICS

Lance and Lucy's grandson Paul, my husband, spent his early childhood in and out the farmhouse kitchen and dairy, nibbling curd from the vat and drinking milk straight from the cow. When we married, these were the poignant conversations we had about the farm. How it had been and what it had now become. I have also had the joy of growing up on a dairy farm, one that has been farmed organically for three decades. My love of territorial cheese has evolved from my love of agriculture. The prefix "agri", meaning a field or pasture, has always struck a chord and I struggled to understand how this controlled indoor environment for our cows was benefitting our cheesemaking.

In 2014 Paul and I had come to a crux in the road, the relationship between the cows and farm was becoming more and more tenuous with that of the vat and cheese. The choices we were making on the farm weren't those that reflected our love and passion for our Cheshire. We were becoming in danger of losing the traditions that made these territorial cheeses what they are. We always knew provenance didn't just start in the cheese dairy, it's always been in the soil, grass and milk – we just needed to return to those foundations. We are both grateful that we were perhaps full of the confidence of youth as we ploughed ahead with these changes despite the resistance from Paul's parents. It was also becoming obvious that the more industrial attitude of the previous generation and the unwillingness to change and evolve was unsurmountable and would mean that we agreed to separate the business, retaining the original land and buildings that Lance and Lucy walked their herd to in the late 1940s. It has felt like, in many ways, we have come full circle.

During this period of change we also built relationships that became friendships with other farmers, cheesemakers and mongers. We were all equally aware that perhaps only half the story was being told in the cheese, that we were – by being encouraged to be more industrial farmers – losing our cheeses' identities. For me it had all felt too prescriptive, too removed from the fields, like we were searching for conversations that would never be spoken. We had found our tasting discussions becoming harder, there just wasn't so much to talk about when the variables of the milk were so controlled. I remember telling a customer that the cheese we made around this area was thanks to the salty Cheshire Plains the cows grazed then realising I had no right to that claim seeing as our cows no longer grazed! I imagine some people may think we were foolish to leap into the unknown with our dramatic changes to our farm. But right from the start it was joyous and incredibly rewarding, far more than we ever hoped. The changes have seen the cows return to graze the pastures; the introduction of more native flowers, grasses and trees; a calving season that gives us an early, mid and late lactation cheese; and more fundamentally has balanced the relationship between farm and dairy.

In December 2020, after a remarkable thirty plus years in the dairy, Gary Gray put one last cheese on the presses. His swansong was not only to make some of the best cheese he had ever produced, but to share his enormous knowledge of the make and all the idiosyncrasies of our dairy. The previous six years had been an exciting time of change and progress on the farm, but they were also years that naturally had a large impact on the cheesemaking, and Gary had not only come along for the ride,

he had shared in our highs and lows. In the last couple of months both Paul and I shadowed Gary as he followed his meticulous routine.

IT ALL STARTS WITH THE MILK

There was never any doubt that Paul would make Cheshire in the dairy his grandma had founded, but although I'm sure he subconsciously felt the weight of her legacy, he has fallen into the rhythm of cheesemaking in his own way. Perhaps he was destined to. For Paul, and ultimately the Cheshire we make, his connection to the farm is pretty unique in 21st century UK cheesemaking. When he first started in the dairy, his day would start with the 5 am milking before he piped the 4,000 litres we needed for the vat. He still says this gives him an enormous head start on the day, for he knows the day's milk, he knows which paddock the cows were grazing, the amount of freshly calved cows and so on.

We use a blend of morning and night milk to help stabilise the fats and proteins. We don't always get it right, but the joy and fascination that comes from how we allow the milk to express itself in the Cheshire is what really matters. To do that you need to have confidence in the make, and much of that bravery comes from confidence in our fresh raw material – milk. It's also about quantities and timings; the handful of starters we rotate, the traditional rennet. All these additions to the vat have an impact, and we will continue to challenge how they function and react. The most significant change to our make took a few years to come to fruition: we visited other territorial makers, particularly Graham Kirkham of Mrs Kirkhams Lancashire Cheese. We read Lucy's notes and other books on Cheshire cheese and, encouraged by Neal's Yard Dairy, began cutting the curd with handheld knives. It doesn't sound like much, but seeing is believing. It is one of my favourite parts of the dairy day, to see the curd gently split into smaller and

smaller pieces as the curd sinks and the heady milky scent is released. This part of the day is serene around the vat, but the wash and pressroom are bustling as all the moulds are scrubbed and the previous day's cheese is bound in calico cloth to be taken to the maturation rooms. The cloth is a very open weave that, once wrapped tightly around the cylindrical cheeses, allows the mould to grow and bloom.

MATURATION: ADDING NUANCES TO A TASTE THAT IS ALREADY THERE

Our maturation rooms are old brick buildings with Napoleonic timbers that used to house cattle before being repurposed. They have a colossal amount of flora and fauna that permeate the cloth as the cheese grow their whiskery mould and ripen. This is where the Cheshires spend the next eight weeks, tucked up on shelves, only disturbed when we rub and turn them to help balance the moisture in the body of the cheese. The moisture that is retained in each crumb of Cheshire should allow it to be giving and soft. To crumble but hold its form when cut, to be juicy without free moisture. I think we have had so many conversations about the texture we have developed a whole set of descriptors for the Cheshire crumble! Another of my favourite times of the week is the boring and note taking of certain batches, the time capsules that keep you guessing until you peel back the cloth. The bore reveals the story of the cheese, and I will never tire of that and the conversations it provokes, especially with mongers and other cheesemakers for whom this is our passion and livelihood. I like to see how much fat is on the back of the iron, to breathe in that instant smell, sometimes cow breath, sometimes citrus fruits. The way the cheese breaks in the palm of your hand and then your mouth. The bite should be a substantial buttery crumble that releases a lemony, grassy, sometimes umami flavour, juicy and long-lasting.

Our Cheshire flavour is certainly nuanced, as is the texture. There are so many elements that influence the end product and, despite the sixty-year heritage, we still have so much to learn both from the past and the future.

We make three kinds of Cheshire, all timeless, traditional British Territorial cheeses made from raw milk and bound in cloth.

Appleby's Cheshire

It has an earthy complexity and a subtleness that lingers. The characteristic crumble is delicate and dewy. By adding annatto to the make, the Appleby's Coloured Cheshire has a warm sunrise colour. It takes around eight weeks to mature.

Appleby's White Cheshire

White Cheshire has a soft milky appearance turning slightly darker at the rind. The characteristic crumble can be more robust, with a delicious citrus length. It also takes around eight weeks to mature. Interestingly, White Cheshire is more likely to be eaten in the North of England.

Appleby's Smoked Cheshire

Small batches of matured Appleby's Coloured Cheshire are smoked over oak. The Smoked Cheshire cheeses are subtle enough to still taste the provenance but have meaty, toasty flavours that are upfront and moreish.

Appleby's Double Gloucester
A classic British Territorial that has been made here at Appleby's Dairy for decades. It has a nutty, rich and buttery flavour and a texture that has more bite. The addition of annatto gives this cheese its bold harvest sun colour. It takes around sixteen weeks to mature.

Paul and I also recently reintroduced the deliciously mellow whey butter after a 30-year interlude. The whey is a by-product of the cheesemaking process that still contains enough solids to be separated into cream. The whey cream is churned and hand patted and the remaining whey is fed to our outdoor pigs or put back on the land.

FUTURE ADVENTURES

Our five children have encouraged us to become even more sustainable. They value the produce and livelihood we have, and their connection to the land is close. In addition to helping with the cows and cheese, they care for the few pigs and sheep and press the apples from the orchard into juice. Our eldest child has spent holidays coppicing the woodland, and all the children have planted trees on the farm. Not only will they offer cover for the herd, but they are an invaluable part of the farm's ecosystem. An ecosystem that we know works better when it has all its component parts. We are aware that our next few years here will be spent investing time in further regeneration of the land so we can sustain the relationship between us, the cows and ultimately our Cheshire cheese.

One of our more recent challenges has been with our stock. The breeding of the cows has changed, and we are seeing the first of our homebred crosses joining the herd. We have moved away from the Holstein Friesian who produced a large volume of milk but who also needed to see a nutritionist, hoof specialist and vet – a lovely and kind cow in general but not one suited to walking along tracks to paddocks at the far end of the farm. We have tried to breed a cow that loves to graze come rain or shine, with a deep belly, sound hooves and a neat udder and teats. A cow that calves and mothers easily, is gentle to handle and produces milk with the right amount of protein and butterfat to make cheese. We have used Danish Red, Montbéliarde and British Friesian to produce a good balance of healthy genetics. It's exciting to see the improvements as the youngstock come into the herd, and lovely to have got to know them as they've grown. We calf outdoors from August. Most cows will find a quiet spot to labour at dawn and, although we're always on hand to check, there is very rarely a need to disturb them. Calving outdoors has been one of the most surprising benefits to cow and calf; it seems (unsurprisingly) everyone is far happier with the space of a large field and the ability to hide in the standing hay they graze. We had forgotten how natural a cow's instinct is. For years we almost ran their lives. There is still more progress in the relationship to be made. We have been looking at the possibility of leaving the calf with mother for a longer period of time, something we are keen to adopt. We have also found we are able to milk once a day at certain times of the year, this again is something we are very much studying and discussing with other farmers – along with topics such as soil health, herbal leys, silvopasture, composting and carbon capturing. So there is still much progress to be made here. We still have constraints, financial worries and the need for more time to study and learn, but it feels wonderful to be on this road.

CONVERSATIONS WITHOUT CONCLUSIONS

For Paul and I, the conversations we have with other farmers, cheesemakers, mongers, scientists, microbiologists, naturalists and anyone who wants to talk about farming and the production of food are of enormous value. There is rarely a conclusion to these discussions where we all sit back and think we've finished. One door leads to another! It is one of the reasons the cheese world is unique – the transparency of these conversations is unusual within businesses so similar. But the sharing of knowledge and the support from those who can understand, empathise and offer help is remarkable. The survival of territorial cheeses like ours relies on the connection with mongers and consumers as we strive to make cheese that is delicious and wholesome, ensuring a future for both farm and family. We love to have people visit the farm and dairy. The interactions span so many types and styles of agriculture and cheesemaking from all over the world, but there is always common ground. We have recently begun to develop a traditional "green fade" or Blue Cheshire, and the conversations as we've hit hurdles have been invaluable and collaborative. Our thanks are to this cheese world who not only provide us with delicious sustenance in the way of other cheeses but also sustain our souls, encourage us when times are hard, challenge us to be bold in our decision making and share in our successes.

IT IS ONE OF THE REASONS THE CHEESE WORLD IS UNIQUE – THE TRANSPARENCY OF THESE CONVERSATIONS IS UNUSUAL WITHIN BUSINESSES SO SIMILAR. BUT THE SHARING OF KNOWLEDGE AND THE SUPPORT FROM THOSE WHO CAN UNDERSTAND, EMPATHISE AND OFFER HELP IS REMARKABLE.

OUR CHESHIRE FLAVOUR IS CERTAINLY NUANCED, AS IS THE TEXTURE. THERE ARE SO MANY ELEMENTS THAT INFLUENCE THE END PRODUCT AND, DESPITE THE SIXTY-YEAR HERITAGE, WE STILL HAVE SO MUCH TO LEARN BOTH FROM THE PAST AND THE FUTURE.

TASTE PROFILE

APPLEBY'S CHESHIRE
Appleby's Dairy

English Cheshire made from cow's milk

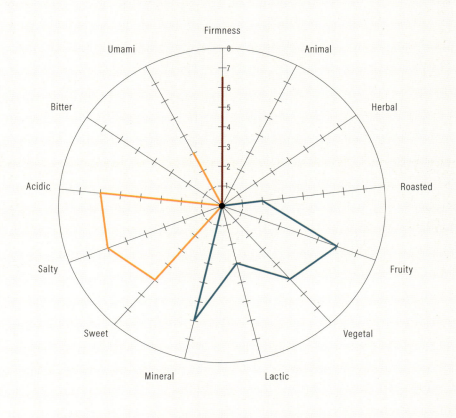

■ texture   ■ aroma   ■ flavour

TEXTURE	**GRAINED AND CRUMBLY**
DOMINANT FLAVOURS	**FLINT, WET ROCK**
	YOGURT, WHEY
	GREEN APPLE, LEMON
	FRESH GRASS
SUBTLE NOTES	**HAZELNUTS**
	ROASTED NUTS
	HEATHER
	MEAT BROTH
	EARTHY TONES
WINE TIPS	**FRESH FRUITY MINERAL WHITE WINE**
	e.g. Chenin Blanc without barrel aging or Grüner Veltliner

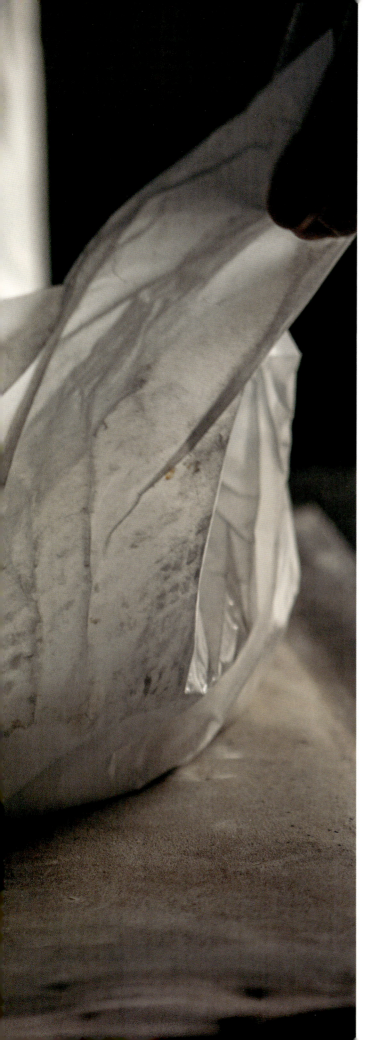

FROMAGERIE DONGÉ

authentic and artisanal Brie de Meaux

CHEESEMAKER

LUC DONGÉ
Fromagerie Dongé
Founded in 1930
Triconville, Meuse
FRANCE

FRANCE'S CHEESE CULTURE

Cheese production in France contributes to its cultural heritage because it's closely connected to a traditional and artisanal savoir-faire. Cheese has been a part of our diet since prehistoric times, and its origins stem from around the same time that animal husbandry was introduced. It is a concentrate of the basic foodstuff milk, with all the quality it contains. Therefore, cheese is a product of human development and civilization, given that it satisfies a human need to conserve milk, an abundant source of protein. Today, the cheesemaking tradition is firmly embedded in French culture, as the country is home to over 90 thousand dairy farms and 3000 cheese dairies, each with their own expertise. We can say that the history of cheese is an inextricable part of France's history, given that many kings and emperors, such as Louis XVI, Charlemagne and Napoleon, all greatly valued the cheeses they discovered on their journeys.

Although the history of cheese is intertwined with French history and tradition, cheese is first and foremost a product of the land, often made in a restricted geographical area and following highly specific methods that are handed down from generation to generation. In France, the various dairy cow breeds and the eight large cheese families result from human choices that have to do with the climate, the geography, and sometimes the geology of a particular area.

As a result, French cheeses evoke a distinct sense of identity and continuity. Historical context, geographical characteristics, reputation and know-how all form the identity of an area or country – hence the implementation of the Protected Designation of Origin (PDO).

French cheeses contribute to cultural diversity and embody human creativity, both for France's cultural heritage and the various communities, which is why we can speak of a true cheese culture in France.

CHEESEMAKERS SINCE 1930

As the Dongé family, we have been in the cheesemaking business for several generations. And, we don't just make any type of cheese; we make Brie de Meaux. In 1930,

OUR CHEESE IS A FAMILY AFFAIR BECAUSE IT IS STILL MADE IN EXACTLY THE SAME WAY AS MY GRANDFATHER ETIENNE MADE IT IN 1922.

Etienne Dongé bought the cheese factory at Triconville, where he had been working since 1922. The production of Emmentaler was replaced by that of brie; the cheese was sold fresh and salted because Dongé was only a cheesemaker and not an affineur at the time. During the war, production was brought to a halt. When activities resumed after the war, the fresh cheeses were sold in the Parisian area to affineurs who allowed the cheeses to mature before selling them under their own brand name. In 1962, Etienne's son, Claude, took over the cheese dairy. He was soon joined by his wife Madeleine, who shared Claude's passion for cheese and gave up her job as a teacher in 1966. The journey they undertook was not without its pitfalls, and they soon realized that they had to start ripening their own cheeses if they wanted to avoid falling by the wayside; that was different altogether! Madeleine and Claude put everything they had into becoming affineurs and setting up their own distribution network for selling their cheeses. Madeleine Dongé became Fromagerie Dongé's sales representative and visited Rungis and other trade fairs.

Their efforts succeeded, and soon my brother Jean-Michel and I started to work in the cheese dairy; he as a cheesemaker, and I as a cheesemonger. We were also forced to innovate, and so every generation has contributed to keeping the tradition alive in its own way. We invested in new production spaces to anticipate future standards and diversify our selection.

But, despite our expansion with new technologies, we continue to stay true to our artisanal production methods and craftsmanship a century later. Our cheese is a family affair because it is still made in exactly the same way as my grandfather Etienne made it in 1922.

A PASSION FOR REAL CHEESE

I always say that it's impossible to ease into the business. You need to work long hours, and you regularly stumble across problems along the way. But all the hardship is quickly forgotten by the satisfaction you get when you see how the milk transforms into a cheese like our Brie de Meaux – a real cheese!

The passion for real cheese that drives Jean-Michel and I has always been a part of us without us realizing it. Our childhood home was situated just 50 meters away from the cheese dairy, and Jean-Michel and I grew up with its sounds: the clanking lids of the milk cans and the smell of milk and apples when the cheeses started to ferment on the shelves. All those impressions, smells and sounds felt like home, even though we didn't realize it at the time.

It wasn't until my parents started ripening our cheeses and selling them at Rungis themselves that I began to open myself up to the world of cheese. It was a wondrous new world. My passion for cheese manifested in 1995 at the *Salon du Fromage.* I was introduced to other cheesemakers and was struck by the welcoming atmosphere, the authenticity of the people, and the values that they all carried with them. It was the cheeses that brought us together, the fruits of our labour that make us all so immensely proud. Our passion for cheese drove each one of us. This passion for the product allows us to preserve our expertise, especially when you can draw from a long family history.

My passion for cheese grew when I was allowed to accompany my mother to the national cheese committee. Gérard Ripaud from the Ministry of Agriculture and Food had invited the proponents of raw milk cheese – milk producers, cheesemakers and affineurs – and government officials to join him. Together, we travelled to Switzerland to view the production of L'Evitaz cheese. As I admired the cheesemaking process, I understood that we were fortunate enough to be working in the world's best profession. That experience has also made me realize that every cheese production process has its own terroir, region, history, and know-how; that all those elements taken together make real cheese. And, that it is essential to commit yourself to preserving, discovering, and above all, maintaining the expertise that gives these cheeses their authenticity. It goes without saying that this passion has never ceased to grow.

TRADITION AND INNOVATION GO HAND IN HAND

As far as I'm concerned, real cheese is made from raw milk. And, as with most simple things in life, this is the hardest to achieve. Preparing cheese with raw milk places stringent demands on every stage of the process: on the production and quality of the milk, on the processing of the milk to cheese, and on the maturation process of the cheese. The production of raw milk

THE CHANGES AIMED NOT TO INCREASE PRODUCTION BUT TO IMPROVE PRODUCTION. WITH THE HELP OF NEW CONTEMPORARY TECHNOLOGIES, WE CAN SAFEGUARD OUR QUALITY WHILE PRESERVING OUR ARTISANAL PRODUCTION METHODS.

cheese poses new challenges every time. Each day of production is different because raw milk cheese is a living product. That's why they are unique from day to day and from season to season. When we make raw milk cheese, we always need to be alert because our expertise is put to the test every single day.

To make real cheese, you need to respect the entire dairy chain and support and guide the farmers to deliver milk of the highest quality. Without good milk, you will never get quality cheese. As a cheesemaker, you also need to concern yourself with the welfare of the animals, the environment, and the people and their health. They are all linked together. And when all these elements are guaranteed, then you can speak of the final product as real cheese.

Jean-Michel and I wish to keep up this tradition, no matter what the cost. But, because we understand that working conditions at the cheese dairy are anything but easy, we combine tradition with modern means. That adventure started in September 2013. It took us over 18 months to move the production over to a new site and give ourselves the time to fine-tune all the parameters. The production spaces in the old building were divided over two floors and were limited in terms of area, which made it difficult to work efficiently. The goal of the move was to improve the organization and working conditions on the floor by having everything take place on the ground floor so that the process would run more smoothly. We thought long and hard about the design of the new building. Jean-Michel and I felt it was important to increase the total surface area (by fifty percent, no less) and to improve the light coming into the space for the employee's comfort and biorhythms. The new production unit is more environmentally friendly as well, much more energy-efficient and better insulated. The cooling installation can also be used, for instance, to heat the water for the bathroom facilities. We did choose to preserve the brick walls in the production spaces, both before and after affinage.

The changes aimed not to increase production but to improve production. With the help of new contemporary technologies, such as electronic regulation of the temperature and humidity in the production hall, we can safeguard our quality while preserving what has been dear to us for three generations: our artisanal production methods. The cheese is still made through natural means and with human hands. We have changed nothing in the way we do things. The tradition from my grandfather's time still holds strong. We've kept all of the old cheesemaking equipment to preserve the microflora.

The large-scale renovations were implemented to retain the essence of our business: to make the famed Brie de Meaux Dongé in the same artisanal way we have done since the cheese dairy started. And how does that work exactly? After filling the hundred-litre vats, rennet is added to the milk. The cheesemakers then cut the curd in a particular way – a family secret – with the help of what we call a *sabre*. Then the curd is carefully ladled into the mould with a brie shovel, a type of perforated skimmer that allows the whey to escape. The draining of the whey occurs naturally. The cheeses are placed in the mould on natural rush mats, so the whey can easily drain away. Once the curds have settled, a second rush mat is placed on top of the cheese. The next day, the cheeses are removed from the moulds and placed on shelves, salted with dry salt and sprayed with penicillin to protect the cheese and allow the crust to develop. The cheeses are then placed in the drying room and left to dry slightly, that is to say: to remove the excess moisture from the cheese and get the maturation process going. We call this the pre-maturation stage. For the second maturation stage, the cheeses are brought to the ripening cellars. We devote a great deal of care to the cheese wheels, which need to be turned over by hand at least once a week until the end of their maturation period to ensure regular consistency. Depending on the season, the cellar temperature, and the humidity, it takes six to eight weeks for the cheese to achieve the desired quality. And then comes the moment when the cellar master selects the cheeses based on the wishes of each client. They are then packaged and shipped to eventually end up on the plates of cheese enthusiasts.

Our passion is so great that we like to expand our assortment with new products. In late 2019, *Le Petit Dongé* was born. This cheese is made from raw milk, just like its big brother, and the production process is the same. However, the taste is different, and this cheese is much creamier when allowed to mature longer. This small brie, weighing some 1.2 kilos, is also available with a filling of black truffle or St. Jean truffle (summer truffle), Indian green pepper, or mustard from Meaux.

Caught up in this creative whirlwind, we also started to work on a recipe from Etienne Dongé to put the leftover cream, which we haven't been using for a long time, to good use. The milk needs to be partially skimmed to make a Brie de Meaux, and the excess cream is of the finest quality because it comes from milk that is also used to prepare a DPO product. This new product is called Barisien, named after our family's hometown,

Bar-le-Duc in the Meuse département. Barisien belongs to the Triple Crème cheese family and is prepared with raw milk. It is a soft cheese enriched with our own fresh cream, with a fuzzy, floury white crust that remains nice and crisp and doesn't dry out and harden after a couple of days. To enjoy its softness and freshness, it's best to eat the cheese when it's still young. But as it matures, the cheese develops its own character, releasing hazelnut and mushroom aromas that accentuate the delicious cream flavour. That's when its creaminess is at its best!

I think there's no mistaking our message: making cheese is our passion!

OUR MESSAGE TO THE CHEESE WORLD

It is essential that we continue to make raw milk cheeses, just like our grandparents used to make them. And ultimately, we bring the fruits of an entire sector's labour – milk suppliers, cheesemakers and affineurs alike – to the consumer's plate. Real cheese must remind our city dwellers of their pastoral and agricultural background because they sometimes tend to forget the hardships and the importance of cultivating land and tending cattle.

I consider myself to be someone who passes on knowledge, who shows how important it is to remember where we come from, and who will not succumb to convenience for convenience's sake. It is therefore immensely rewarding when customers congratulate us on the quality of our cheese.

I believe it is vital to protect the diversity of our dairy products, retain the microbial diversity in our raw milk cheeses, and safeguard the health of future generations – but that brings us to a topic for another day, namely that of the health benefits of raw milk.

I hope that future cheesemakers will understand the artisanal values that we have been championing for decades and that they will continue to stand up for those values – which will one day become their own. Cheese culture must be handed down from generation to generation so that real cheese can continue to exist!

To conclude, I would like to add that aside from our own cheeses, which always grace our table at home, I am a huge fan of other cheeses. I have a soft spot for L'Evitaz, the most distinguished of mountain cheeses. It is only produced between May and October and has a somewhat fine, creamy and supple consistency and a highly aromatic and subtle fruity flavour. But to be honest, I love all European cheeses with a PDO designation. Every one of those cheeses has a unique story to tell. One of my favourite moments of the year is when I return from the *Salon du Fromage* and sit down with my friends to a majestic cheeseboard laden with the finest French and European cheeses. Cheese is synonymous with hospitality, companionship and authenticity. Real cheese takes us on a journey and tells us the story of a specific place. There is nothing better than discovering all those flavours together, accompanied by a fine bottle of wine, preferably white, and united by a shared passion for cheese!

TASTE PROFILE

BRIE DE MEAUX
Fromagerie Dongé

French brie made from cow's milk

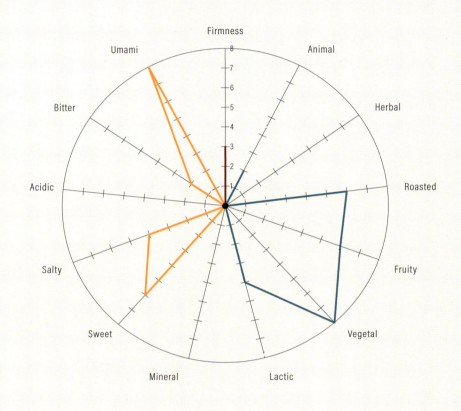

TEXTURE	**SOFT, STICKY AND RUNNY**
DOMINANT FLAVOURS	**MUSHROOMS, WET HAY AND HUMUS**
	HAZELNUTS
	ROASTED WALNUTS
	SMOKED DAIRY PRODUCTS
SUBTLE NOTES	**CREAM**
	CARAMELISED BUTTER
	MEAT BROTH
WINE TIPS	**FRUITY RED WINE WITH FEW OR SUPPLE TANNINS**
	e.g. Pinot Noir or Merlot

JOSEPH PACCARD

artisanal maturation of raw milk Reblochon

CHEESE AFFINEUR

JOSEPH PACCARD
Joseph Paccard SARL
Founded in 1990
Manigod, Haute-Savoie
FRANCE

WWW.REBLOCHON-PACCARD.FR

IN THOSE DAYS, THE FARMERS ONLY MILKED SOME OF THEIR COWS IN ORDER TO PAY FEWER TAXES. THE REMAINING MILK (AFTER TAXES), A SECOND MILKING ALSO KNOWN AS "REBLOCH," WAS USED TO PRODUCE A CREAMY CHEESE NAMED REBLOCHON.

FRENCH CHEESE CULTURE

Saying that French cheese culture has a long history is an understatement! Animal husbandry in France dates back to more than 12,000 years ago. Milk and cheese have been essential ingredients for centuries, preceding the introduction of bread and wine. Nonetheless, it took hundreds of years before the first farm cheeses were produced towards the end of the Middle Ages. Back then, every cheese was a raw-milk farmhouse cheese. So, it might be superfluous to point out that pasteurised cheeses have only been around for 150 years.

The first cheeses produced in the 13th century in the Haute-Savoie region served a dual purpose: to feed the farmer and his family and to trade at the local markets. In those days, the famous Reblochon cheese with its unique origins first made its appearance. The farmers rented their lands from a landlord who visited the farm several times each year to collect taxes on the milk produced at the farm. In those days, the farmers only milked some of their cows in order to pay fewer taxes. The remaining milk (after taxes), a second milking also known as "rebloch," was used to produce a creamy cheese named Reblochon.

> I CHOSE THE PRODUCERS OF REBLOCHON BASED ON THEIR HUMAN QUALITIES – MORE SPECIFICALLY, ON HOW CAREFULLY THEY TENDED TO THEIR CATTLE.

Today, there are 800 Reblochon producers, 20% of whom still milk and produce cheese twice a day at the farm; the rest collect the milk once a day. Reblochon was given the AOC (Appellation d'Origine Contrôlée, or controlled designation of origin) designation in 1958, limiting the region of origin to Haute-Savoie in France. Later, other cheeses were discovered, such as the Tomme, a one-and-a-half-kilogram cheese made from pressed, uncooked paste. Before it became the famed Tomme de Savoie with a grey rind, it was called "Tomme Blanche." It was eaten before it had a chance to mature, often with pepper, potatoes and garlic.

Other cheeses were produced from the 10th century onwards when the monks started gathering in monasteries, as was the case in the Abondance Valley. The cows there are also called Abondance; hence, the cheese made from their milk was given the same name. The size of the cheese, weighing about eight or nine kilograms each, is directly linked to the harsh wintry circumstances in elevations above 1000 metres: the cheese was able to ripen for several months before being sold in the cities.

A SAVOYARD FAMILY

I worked as a farmer until 1972 when I became the director of a local cooperative and responsible for the maturation of farmhouse cheeses and non-farmhouse cheeses. In 1990, I returned to my native village of Manigod in Haute-Savoie to establish my own affinage centre with maturation cellars. The business still carries my name, although these days I share my cellars with my sons, Jean-François and Bertrand. In fact, we are twelve Savoyards that form a tight-knit family that is proud of its roots and is focused on the best of what our generous region has to offer.

It wasn't until I turned fifty that I decided to dedicate myself solely to maturing farmhouse cheeses from a strict selection of cheesemakers. Most of them were producers of Reblochon cheeses, and I chose them based on their human qualities – more specifically, on how carefully they tended to their cattle. This may not seem crucial or even complex, but it's the various tiny details and seemingly less critical aspects that contribute to the quality and final cheese product. They make the difference between a standard white cheese and a cheese that evolves into a beautiful, flavourful cheese. By fully dedi-

cating myself to maturing cheeses with the utmost care, I soon became part of a group of cheesemakers who were active in the mountain region – my native village, Manigod, is situated in the Northern Alps close to Chamonix and Lake Annecy – and so I could play my part in preserving this traditional craft and culinary heritage.

We select the cheeses according to the tastes and preferences of our customers. We not only mature Reblochon cheese, but also other typical farmhouse cheeses from the Savoie region, such as Manigodine, Tomme de Savoie, Tome de Bauges, Raclette, Persille de Tignes, Blues, Termignon, Abondance and Beaufort, as well as several goat and sheep cheese varieties.

THE TASTE OF THE ALPS

Over the years, I have developed a personal work method where the varying conditions of the maturation cellars influence the final product. Thankfully, I have been able to share this knowledge with my two sons, Jean-François and Bertrand, so this expertise is safeguarded for the future. We share the same ambition and vision to raise the work of artisanal cheesemakers to the next level. From the beginning, the goal was to maximise the level of creaminess, flavour, attractiveness and typical appearance during the Reblochon maturation process. That is why I make sure that the result of such painstaking work and experienced craftsmanship always ends up with the right cheesemongers, namely small, reliable cheesemongers and local markets. That is how we can be sure that our cheeses meet the high expectations of our critical customers.

Time and patience are two crucial aspects of the cheese maturation process that make all the difference. They are a source of endless fascination to me when it comes to understanding how they optimise flavour and texture in a unique natural product such as farmhouse cheese. In that respect, Reblochon is one of the most difficult cheeses to make and mature. Therefore, it is a great challenge to give flavour and shape to a potential first-class product from my natural environment. Thanks to our cellars, where the humidity, temperature and bacteria levels are constantly monitored, our respect for a traditional

and natural ripening process always takes precedence over hygienic demands. Moreover, the entire cheesemaking process is a fully integrated whole, from the state of the milk as a raw material to the finished cheese, because we constantly monitor and evaluate our relationships with our suppliers and customers.

Real cheese is made from raw milk, a unique raw material in which the state of the milk is not altered through any thermal treatment. Raw milk cheese is always made from milk that isn't heated above 40°C, so it retains all of its original flavour aspects. This guarantees the distinctive character of the terroir and the cattle breed as well as allowing the milk and the resulting final cheese to retain the characteristics of the original ecosystem in which the milk was produced. Under those conditions, cheesemakers and affineurs can guarantee the richness of biodiversity in cheese. Those aspects give artisanal farmhouse cheeses their distinctiveness and character and fascinate me as an affineur.

The Alpine pastures, with their own typical vegetation, provide that guarantee, as do the distinctive cattle breeds native to the mountains, which have adapted to its elevation, climate, landscape, vegetation and nutrition. Those are all features that give the terroir its distinguishing characteristics. That is why only a limited number of cattle breeds, such as Abondance, Tarine and Montbélliarde, are eligible for the production of typical AOC Savoyard cheeses, including Reblochon. The Alpine character of cheese dairies and the pastures at higher elevations provide a unique context for this cheese. From mid-May until autumn, the cheesemakers move to the mountain plateaus with their herds. That's where the grass is extra rich in vitamins and minerals and where meadow flowers create a unique mountain perfume. The cheesemakers make the "same" cheese as they did in their dairies in the valley, but under different circumstances, giving those cheeses a unique character. That is why we can speak of an age-old agropastoral system that preserves the ecological balance when exploiting mountain pastures, an essential condition for agriculture in the Savoie region. This requires a community of 220 to 250 herders in active service and the dedication of 25 to 30 Alpine cooperative cheesemakers.

BY HAND AND WITH FEELING

I feel that the maturation of cheese, just like the making of cheese, is a personal process. It is a craft that you learn to master over the years and it shapes your personality and identity. The cheeses develop their own character, and that is precisely why the arsenal of cheeses that we know today are so unique and distinctive. Making and maturing cheese is not a self-explanatory process. It is an intensive affair that not only requires knowledge and expertise but, equally important, a sense of flair and intuition. I have dedicated a large part of my professional career to the maturation of cheeses. First, I got to know the herds of cattle on the family farm. Getting in touch with nature, the surroundings and the terroir

was an excellent starting point. Over the years, I also got to know the producers. I'm referring to some thirty producers in the Thônes valley who make cheeses on their farms and small artisanal producers in Haute-Savoie who make their own cheese using traditional methods. I still share their joy in seeing how their patience and dedication give cheese its flavour and shape every day.

It is no mean feat to produce Reblochon twice a day, seven days a week under often difficult circumstances. It not only requires energy and knowledge but, above all, a healthy dose of dedication. The cows are milked twice a day, in the mountains in the summer and later in the valley. The raw milk is then curdled in cheese vats, where the curd is stirred and cut. Once the curds are large enough and sink to the bottom, they are poured into cheese moulds by hand before being levelled and lightly pressed. The casein stamp is then applied to the cheese: green for the farmstead Reblochon versus red for the coop Reblochon. The cheeses are then turned and individually stored with a cheese weight on the top to press them lightly.

Everything takes place by hand and with feeling so that the Reblochons-to-be shape into fine cheeses. It is precisely those meticulous actions that form the basis of the cheese-making process that continues to evolve in the draining and drying rooms. After eight to ten days, the Reblochons leave the farm and are moved to our maturation cellars, where we leave the cheeses to mature and develop their flavour. Over several weeks, the cheeses in our cellars are given our undivided attention. They are washed and turned in a precisely determined rhythm and under the most carefully orchestrated circumstances, where the humidity and temperature in the cellars play a central role. During that time, the cheeses pass through our hands some 25 times and develop their typical colour and texture – and ultimately their highly characteristic and distinctive aroma and flavour. Thankfully, the Reblochon terroir has had AOC status since 1958, which

has helped to highlight and preserve that distinguishing character, making it one of the first cheeses to be clearly described and defined as such; a fact that recognises and values the exceptionally distinctive nature of the cheese and the work of the cheesemakers and affineurs.

MY FAVOURITE CHEESES

My favourite cheese is, and will always be, the farmhouse Reblochon. With its unique flavour and typical character, this is a cheese that speaks for itself and proves its exceptional quality time and time again through its subtle aromas. The delicate crust and soft, distinctive flavour make the cheese highly accessible. Reblochon goes perfectly well with a fine Belgian blonde beer or a light Savoie wine that brings the cheese's aroma to the foreground. For me, a farmhouse Reblochon with its unique character is a must on every cheese board. After all, Reblochon is a true joy to experience.

Another unique cheese that I consider one of my favourites is a farmhouse raclette cheese. This cheese is produced high in the Alps on the farm in the summer using raw milk. After four months, the cheese reveals the aromas of the Alpine pastures when it's melted. Although this is quite a fatty cheese, it doesn't release any oils as it melts. The cheese is a delicious accompaniment to potatoes, meat products and white wine from the Savoie region. Anyone who has tasted a Paccard farmhouse raclette cheese has been introduced to a slice of highly rich Savoyard heritage made using ancient production techniques that have been perfected over time. We have only been making and maturing Alpine pasture farmhouse raclette cheese for ten years, but the results each year prove once again the ability of our cheesemakers to adapt to different production methods to bring out the best in the cheese. You can really taste the authentic local heritage in this cheese.

Another favourite is Beaufort, a cheese made in Alpine chalets that is at least two years old. This cheese has been around for centuries, and its concave form is reminiscent of the many stories linked to the complexity and challenges of keeping cattle in Alpine pastures at elevations of 1500 to 2000 metres. The cheese is a true gem when it has reached its full potential in the summer. It is so complex that Beaufort can only be tasted after 18 months and even then, it will not have reached its full flavour potential and have released its fruity aromas. Only after two years of ripening at low temperatures can one taste the rare aromas of exotic fruit and enjoy its remarkably fatty and buttery texture. Only champagne of the highest quality can do justice to this cheese, also known as the Prince of Gruyères. Only 14 cheesemakers in the Alps make these large, 40-kilo cheeses twice a day in the summer. Thanks to their hard work, we can taste the richness of the culinary Savoyard heritage passed down from generation to generation.

BACK TO THE LAND

Every day, I am honoured to be a part of the cheese world. It is almost impossible to comprehend the changes that have taken place over the past 30 years regarding the number of cheeses one can find in cheese shops and how that assortment is presented. The introduction of the AOC designation has resulted in an immense boost to improving the quality of these cheeses and in raising the work that we do to a higher level, from farming to selling.

There is, of course, still much work to be done. I believe that bringing people back to the land to produce more cheese will be the next main step. I feel it is essential to preserve the meadows and fields, because it is the uniqueness of the grass that makes it possible to produce cheeses with such distinctive flavours. The processing of raw milk will continue to be a spearhead and will be our most important task for the future. My mission is to bring people together to think about and exchange ideas on how we can find a feasible bacterial strain (of which a few are being produced today) that can show how beneficial a raw milk cheese is and how rich such a cheese is for human consumption.

Finally, we must always keep the bigger picture in mind and remind ourselves that today's cheese world has become what it is thanks to the commitment of many people who could probably have chosen a much easier and more profitable path in life but instead chose to dedicate their lives to something bigger than themselves. Being part of the cheese world is believing in a world where people share communal values, carry out projects, build farms and maturation cellars, work on a better product for now and in the future, and preserve a valued heritage so that we may pass it down to future generations.

TASTE PROFILE

REBLOCHON
Joseph Paccard SARL

French soft cheese made from cow's milk

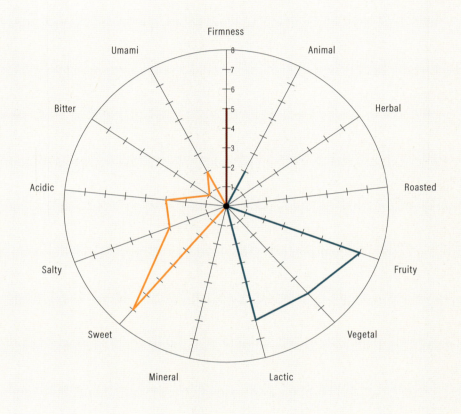

TEXTURE	**SUPPLE, SPRINGY AND SMOOTH**
DOMINANT FLAVOURS	**NUTS**
	FLOWERS, HEATHER
	CREAM
SUBTLE NOTES	**EARTH, HUMUS AND MUSHROOMS**
	HAY
	CITRUS
WINE TIPS	**LIGHT, FRESH AND FRUITY RED WINE**
	e.g. Gamay
	LIGHT, FRESH WHITE WINE
	e.g. Pinot Blanc or Chardonnay without barrel aging

TASTE PROFILE | # BEAUFORT HAUT ALPAGE AOP
Groupement Pastoral de Plan Pichu

French hard mountain cheese from Haute-Savoie made from cow's milk

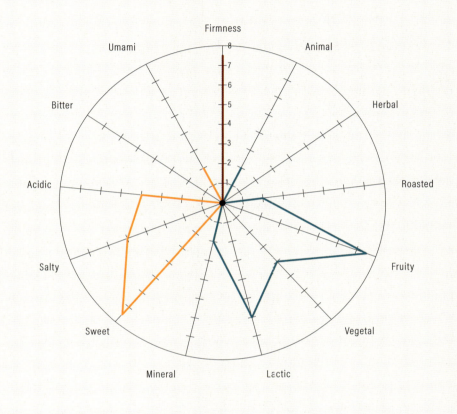

■ texture   ■ aroma   ■ flavour

TEXTURE	**FIRM AND SLIGHTLY GRAINED**
DOMINANT FLAVOURS	**FLOWERS, HONEY** **HEATHER** **HERBS** **BUTTER** **NUTS**
SUBTLE NOTES	**STRAW, HAY** **GRASS** **WET WOOL**
WINE TIPS	**COMPLEX WHITE WINE WITH FLORAL TONES** e.g. Chenin Blanc or a blend of Marsanne, Rousanne or Viognier **COMPLEX WHITE WINE WITH SOME BARREL AGING** e.g. blend of white Bordeaux (Sauvignon Blanc and Sémillon) with some barrel aging

MAISON MONS

in search of the best traditional cheeses

CHEESE AFFINEUR

HERVÉ MONS
Maison Mons
Founded in 1970
Pré Normand in Saint-Haon-le-Châtel
Loire
FRANCE

WWW.MONS-FROMAGES.COM

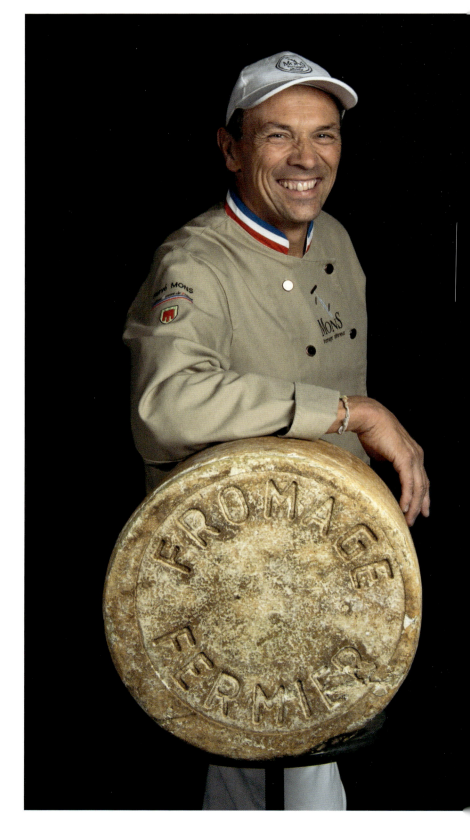

TOUR DE FRANCE

France is renowned worldwide as the land of cheese. It owes that reputation to the exceptional richness and diversity of its soils (terroirs), where climatological circumstances have given rise to creativity and diversity. I have been a fervent terroir advocate ever since I first started in the field in the 1980s.

My family's cheese story began in 1964 when my parents decided to start selling cheese at the markets in Roanne. The 1970s were prosperous; the business grew and became a fixture in the region. When I was about 16 years old, I started working in the family business. I embarked on an actual Tour de France to learn the trade and, during those years, I worked with the best French cheesemakers around at the time. Over the course of that learning period, not only did I learn about everything from the production to the ripening and marketing of cheese, but I also got to know many people. In 1983, I opened the business's first permanent store in the Halles Diderot in the heart of Roanne. The number of stores has only increased since then.

MORE THAN ONE BUSINESS

Maison Mons: they are actually different businesses. We currently have 15 stores scattered across the country. We have two cheese dairies where we process organic raw milk from cows, goats and sheep. Our dairies use the Obsalim method, and the animals are only given feed crops and grass to eat. We also have various ripening centres. First, we have a centre in Perpezat with an assortment of cheeses that are solely made with raw milk from Salers cows. Second, there is the Collogne tunnel in Ambierle, an old railway tunnel that we converted into a modern and efficient ripening cellar. And finally, there are the ripening cellars of Saint Haon le Châtel, built according to a unique and innovative concept that is currently being patented. In concrete terms, this means that we always have about 250 cheeses in our ripening cellars and a direct link to about 130 suppliers. In 2005, together with my brother Laurent, I established *Mons Formation*, an educational institute specializing in the maturation and marketing of dairy products. The goal is to share and pass on our expertise in cheese culture to as many people as possible – in France and beyond. So, we are very proud that our cheeses are sold in more than 30 countries worldwide: from the United States to Italy, Sweden, and even Japan.

In short, after decades of work, innovation and investment, my brother and I have built a business where work is a pleasure and one that integrates the three elements that make up our craft: milk, production and sales. I continue to be amazed every day at what we can still achieve!

THE ALCHEMY OF CHEESE

My passion for real cheese has developed over time and stems both from my curiosity and from the need to understand all the subtleties involved in creating a quality cheese. Each new discovery opens new doors, and the alchemy of cheese seems limitless. That only serves to foster my passion.

The quality of the cheese is paramount to me. With every cheese, my goal is to understand how the producer makes the cheese, what the circumstances look like, what know-how is involved, and how the cheesemaker succeeds in controlling most of the parameters in their ecosystem to maintain that cheese's quality. The rapport, transparency, and human relationships that develop during the collaboration between cheesemaker and affineur are essential.

Once you know what you want to achieve through your work, you also know where to start. For me, that starting point is finding the best cheeses and taking them to the next level by ripening them and offering them to my customers. If you have made the right choice, you are rewarded with the satisfaction of a job well done and loyal customers. That's one of the reasons I'm very proud that I was awarded the *Meilleur Ouvrier de France* (MOF) title in 2000.

THREE FAVOURITE CHEESES

1. Salers Tradition from raw cow's milk

This is really an exceptional cheese that continues to amaze us in every phase of its production. It reminds me of the most demanding cheesemaking tradition, a true mountain cheese that our friend and young supplier, Géraud Delorme, maintains at the highest level. The taste profile of Salers Tradition is relatively atypical; it's a cheese with a rustic character. You initially taste salt, but that quickly gives way to a highly intense aromatic complexity. It's meaty, with the warm aroma of the barn, yet herbal, with an infusion of hay and a fresh bitterness reminiscent of gentian. Salers Tradition is truly unique and leaves no one unmoved.

What makes Salers Tradition so unique?

Although we wish to illustrate in this book how diverse the assortment of real cheese is and we don't wish to single out one single cheese as being truly unique, Salers Tradition comes very close. It epitomizes the simplicity of real cheese: Salers Tradition is a cheese that tells the story of how soil, animals and flavour are intertwined like no other. And we feel that deserves an explanation here.

Salers is 100% *fermier* or farmhouse cheese. The cheese is made from the raw milk of grazing cows. The raw milk is immediately processed after milking in a chestnut cheese vat. Salers is made between 1 May and 31 October during the grazing period. Outside this period, the milk is processed into Cantal cheese. For convenience's sake, you could say that Salers is a Cantal, but it's a Cantal *fermier*, which means that it is a more aromatized type of Cantal than the pasteurized version. Salers has more complex aromas than Cantal and can contain hints of herbs, spices, hay, nuts, citrus fruits, butter, cream and even a meaty character with a smoky touch. Salers can be distinguished from Cantal by a red aluminium plaque embedded into the crust.

Salers Tradition is a Salers's milk cheese and therefore the milk must come from Salers cows. This breed will only allow itself to be milked when the calf is still with the mother. Salers cows guarantee rich, aromatic milk. When you buy Salers Tradition, you're supporting the additional effort it takes to work with this breed as opposed to easier and more productive breeds. To give an indication: a Salers cow gives, in addition to what she feeds her calf, about 8 litres of milk, whereas a Montbéliarde cow may produce 20 litres and a Holstein 30 litres. There are currently only five producers of Salers Tradition cheese.

Salers belongs, together with Cantal and Laguiole, to the larger Cheddar family, and the three cheeses are all produced in the same way. The milk is heated to 32°C and curdled. The curd is cut into small pieces to drain off the whey and is then gathered into a compact mass which is then pressed in its entirety to remove all the whey. This is followed by a typical phase in the process: the ripening of the curd so the lactic bacteria have room to develop. This gives the cheese its characteristic flavour. The ripened curd is then broken down, salted and poured into moulds. The curd is pressed a second time in the moulds. Over the course of two days, the last drops of whey are squeezed out, and the cheese settles into its final shape. Finally, the moulds are removed, and the cheese is transferred to the ripening cellars. Young Cantal takes one to two months to ripen, the *entre deux* matures between three to six months, and aged Cantal is at least six months old. The ripening of Salers takes place over a minimum of three months and a maximum of a year. Laguiole has an even longer ripening period: at least 8 to a maximum of 12 months.

Salers, Cantal and Laguiole all vie for the title of the "oldest cheese in France" and are also the forerunners of the English Cheddar. The recipe was probably introduced in the United Kingdom by the Romans after a stay in Cantal. One thing that the three cheese varieties do not have in common is their Protected Designation of Origin (PDO). The designation varies per cheese, and this means that the rules are different for each cheese. Cantal and Laguiole are produced year-round, whereas Salers may only be produced when the cows are grazing in the fields. Salers and Laguiole may only be made with raw milk; pasteurized milk may be used for Cantal, which is why it has the highest production levels.

2. Plancherin d'Arêches from raw goat's milk

The Plancherin d'Arêches is the result of our close collaboration with Caroline Joguet, a young goat farmer from the Savoy region. The cheese is inspired by various existing processes, but the recipe is unique. You can position this cheese somewhere between Reblochon and Vacherin, very subtle with a delightful aroma that holds its own between meaty and woody.

3. Mistralou from raw goat's milk

If ever an exceptional goat's cheese existed, this would be it! Francois and Vanessa Masto produce this cheese, which is made from the milk of Rove goats that wander over the mountains around the village of Simiane la Rotonde, not far from Banon. This gem of a cheese is created through lactic acid production, without fermentation, solely by reusing the whey as a starter. The cheese is wrapped in a chestnut leaf and ripened for several weeks in the cellar. The result is a creamy cheese with just the right amount of goat flavour and a refined, woody aroma.

EXCHANGING KNOWLEDGE

My hope for the future is to pass on and continue all the hard work that has been done over the years to keep our sector alive for the farmers, the cheesemakers, the affineurs and the customers. I believe that we should hand our expertise down to a new generation and educate them in the craft. The most significant barriers are primarily of a hygienic nature because raw milk does not meet current food hygiene standards. But second, the raw milk approach requires dedication and reflection from all actors, from the field to the plate. So, if I were to say one thing to the cheese world, it's always to remain curious and keep tasting, understanding, exchanging and sharing.

MAISON MONS

TASTE PROFILE | # SALERS TRADITION
Maison Mons

French hard cheese made from cow's milk

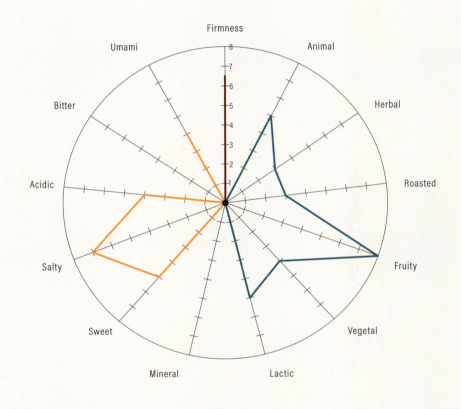

texture · aroma · flavour

TEXTURE	**FIRM AND STICKY**
DOMINANT FLAVOURS	**FLOWERS**
	HAZELNUTS, WALNUTS
	BUTTERMILK, YOGURT, CREAM
	GRASS
SUBTLE NOTES	**CITRUS**
	HAY
	SPICES (NUTMEG)
	SMOKED MEAT
WINE TIPS	**WHITE WINE WITH SMOKEY TONES**
	e.g. Pinot Gris
	SPICY RED WINE WITH FEW OR VERY SUPPLE TANNINS
	e.g. Syrah

JASPER HILL FARM

hand-crafted European-style cheeses made in the US

CHEESEMAKER

MATEO AND ANDY KEHLER
Jasper Hill Farm
Founded in 2003
Greensboro, Vermont
UNITED STATES OF AMERICA

WWW.JASPERHILLFARM.COM

AMERICAN CHEESE CULTURE

America is one of the world's largest consumers of cheese. Unfortunately, much of the cheese we eat is produced in industrial settings that bear no resemblance to the small creameries that once dotted our nation's countryside. The infiltration of these standardized, uniform blocks of cheese into our homes and grocery stores began in the mid-century, amidst a technological boom that allowed us to use modern science to extend the shelf life of various food products for our troops abroad. It wasn't long before we applied this cutting-edge approach to everyday mainstream products. These synthesized, sterile so-called foods had broad appeal: they were cheaper, less perishable and more consistent than fresh ingredients.

This new approach to food production quickly became the norm, but by the seventies, a yearning to reconnect with the land was beginning to emerge. On the West coast, new restaurants prioritized the use of fresh, seasonal ingredients, sparking a radical return to real food that would ripple eastward. Simultaneously, American chefs were becoming increasingly well-travelled and introducing diners to an ever-widening range of imported delicacies. As our appetite for European-style products ballooned alongside our desire for locally sourced ingredients, an opportunity for artisan cheese to make its comeback opened up.

The American Artisan Cheese Movement began when several pioneering women climbed through this window of opportunity and ambitiously established small creameries of their own across the country. As they earnestly produced tiny batches of French-inspired goat's cheese, they filled a budding niche for American-made, European-style cheeses, growing loyal followings among regional culinary circles. The number of small-scale American cheesemakers grew slowly until the 90s, when we saw a sudden boom in artisan cheese production. Since then, dozens of new creameries have ushered hundreds of uniquely American cheeses onto the market, many earning national and international acclaim at the highest levels. There are nearly one thousand artisan cheesemakers in this country today.

Since the inception of the Farm to Table movement, American consumers have developed a deeper understanding of the ways in which our food system works against local agricultural communities. We are seeing more and more domestic cheeses in specialty shops and on restaurant menus in response to these shifting stand-

ever-more diverse and thriving agricultural tradition in the Northeast Kingdom – one that is able to create a regional identity for the product developed to suit our region, culture, and ambitions for a sustainable future.

A TASTE OF PLACE

Cheese is primordial. It has spurred and fed human civilisation from the Fertile Crescent and the inception of agriculture through the building of Empire and beyond the Industrial Revolution. In its simplest form, cheesemaking is the aggregation and preservation of protein; in its highest form, cheesemaking is alchemy. With only four ingredients but 1,000 iterations, every cheese embodies the particulars of history: the texture of place and people.

Cheese can reflect a natural economy and the highest expression of a working landscape, or an industrial plasticine product made from fragments of milk at scales that impose an economy beyond a landscape's capacity to survive it. We eschew the latter. Every aspect of our operation is carefully, constantly managed in the name of preserving our signature taste of place. By focusing our efforts on maintaining the health of our soils and diversifying our pastures, we have been able to create the conditions necessary for our cows to produce the rich, high-quality milk needed for cheesemaking.

The painstaking measures we take to manage our land and our herds result in raw milk with remarkable microbial diversity. As our milk undergoes its transformation into cheese, we aim to preserve this microflora, harnessing its potential to develop complex flavours over time. As we ripen our cheeses in their carefully calibrated vaults, these flavours continue to deepen and evolve, further distilling our terroir into every wheel.

IT ALL BEGINS WITH SUNSHINE AND SOIL

We started Jasper Hill Farm to satisfy three intrinsic needs: meaningful work in a place that we love, with people we love. Greensboro, population 762, is nestled in the hills of Vermont's Northeast Kingdom. For 97 years, Greensboro and the shores of Caspian Lake have been the happy place of our collective family childhood. The landscape here is defined by the pastoral beauty of the farmer's footprint on the land. For generations, farmers have scratched a living from the hills here, milking cows in summer, cutting timber in the winter and tapping maple trees to produce maple syrup in the spring.

But Vermont is not a low-cost producer of anything and, like rural communities across the US and the world, the industrialization of agriculture and the vagaries of globalized commodity markets have decimated our local agricultural economy and led to the slow outward migration of young people, the greying of our community, and a decline that has been ongoing for nearly 100 years. Agricultural policy in the US has effectively transferred wealth from rural communities to urban and suburban populations through pricing mechanisms. By incentivizing overproduction and driving scale in the never-ending quest for greater and greater efficiency, dairy farming has become barely recognizable. It is no longer feasible to graze cows on most farms – the fields and pastures are turned over, and genetically engineered corn grows on sloped ground. Water quality is degraded, soil lost, and equity is transferred from the balance sheets of farmers to the only beneficiaries of this system, consumers, who have come to rely on cheap food, ignorant to the violence of its externalized costs.

Highly processed products line the shelves of our grocery stores, widening the chasm between consumers and their local farming communities. The globalized economy has degraded our collective ability to accept the seasonality of agricultural products, and customers have grown accustomed to an unnatural degree of uniformity and stability in their foodstuffs. Small family farms can no longer compete with the convenience, consistency, and low prices that large stores are able to offer; the reckless and short-sighted choices that consumers make to save their own time and money will ultimately cost those small family farms their livelihood.

Jasper Hill is our response to Globalization. In an age of synthetic collateralized debt obligations and a virtual economy divorced from natural laws and limits, at a time when the extractive efficiency of capitalism and its compounding capacity to concentrate wealth threatens to collapse the planet's natural systems, Jasper Hill is our reminder that all capital originates with sunshine and soil. Cheese is a form of capital, a store of value that increases in value over time and is the founding capital of banking systems. The Cheese Cellar is a bank. We take cheese, a distillate of grass, the product

of sunshine, and put it away, deep underground where it increases in value over time and becomes more delicious. In this underground economy, we are the multipliers who concentrate real wealth produced by real people from real places.

Jasper Hill is the collective sum of the people working hard to produce world class cheese. Together we manage 1,000 acres of grass, making cheese seven days a week from the milk produced on our farm and on the farms of four neighbours. We ripen cheese from six cheese makers for whom we manage marketing, sales and distribution. We have built a pipeline to communities with plenty of disposable income into which we feed high-value delicious cheese, and in exchange we extract capital from those communities and redistribute it in a way that commodity markets don't.

Our mission is to plug as many acres within a 15-mile radius as possible into the market we are building. In this way we are able to pay our neighbours for the true value of their labour and their milk. Cheese is a vehicle that helps ensure that young people and families can find a future and make a life in this beautiful place. It is a way to ensure that our local store, our school and the civic infrastructure that supports community can survive for generations to come. Cheese is a powerful force for good.

In a world in which there is so little that is authentic, we offer consumers the opportunity to connect with something real. We create the ecological conditions for deliciousness to emerge. The microbial ecology of raw milk is the sum of the practices on a farm. We harness farming systems and a philosophy to create complexity by embracing practices that produce microbial and human diversity. And we support and defend these traditional practices by harnessing modern scientific technologies to understand and untangle the knowledge that our predecessors intuited. Sunshine, banked in the form of cheese, held in darkness until that light

captured in summer is revealed in the form of a thousand aromas, textures and flavours in an echo of our primordial past.

AWARD-WINNING CHEESE

Our raw milk cheeses offer the purest expression of our signature taste of place. So much of our labour is poured into managing our soil, developing our pastures, drying our hay, and caring for our animals. As we tend to each of these essential aspects of our operation, what we are really doing is farming microbes on a grand scale. We selectively encourage the growth of beneficial microflora, taking care to preserve our native cultures in the name of terroir. As we ripen these cheeses in our caves, we further concentrate their clarity and complexity of flavour. In each batch of cheese, a different day is captured. Bayley Hazen Blue is one of our longest-made and most terroir-driven cheeses. From a technical standpoint, it is our most challenging cheese to make and ripen, but against all odds it manages to be our most consistently delicious cheese. Bayley's success hinges on the quality of our raw milk, and every step of the process demands immense patience and focus. The density of its pillowy curds and the way they are scooped into their individual moulds are crucial to the cheese's texture and the development of even veins, and the uniformity of every hand-spiked opening is what creates consistent bluing. Each wheel is hand-salted, turned and wrapped. The practised technique of our cheesemakers and affineurs is evident in every batch.

The result of this painstaking labour of love is an award-winning cheese that has the ability to transport you to this incredible place that we call home. At first bite, a perfume of the diverse grasses, flowers, and herbs that make up our lush pastures bursts forth. A frosty, felted rind, redolent of the earthy, mineral-rich aromatics in our caves, gently encases each marbled wheel. The richness of our milk coats the palate, leaving a long, sweet-cream finish lingering on the tongue. Months of maturation yield an immersive multi-sensory experience, a crystal-clear distillation of our taste of place. Bayley Hazen Blue serves as proof that American artisan cheesemakers can, in fact, produce cheeses that are able to compete with and even triumph over the European icons they strive to emulate. Bayley Hazen Blue is evidence that we have succeeded in our mission to uphold traditional practices while continuing to innovate. It is a tangible token of our commitment to meaningful work in a place that we love.

09.11.25

09.11.25

TASTE PROFILE

BAYLEY HAZEN BLUE
Jasper Hill Farm

American blue cheese with a natural crust, made from raw cow's milk and indigenous cultures of blue flora

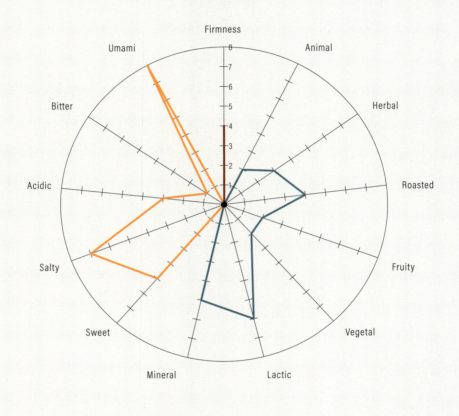

■ texture ■ aroma ■ flavour

TEXTURE	**FIRM AND SMOOTH**
DOMINANT FLAVOURS	**SWEET CREAM** **ANISE** **FRESH OYSTERS**
SUBTLE NOTES	**SHERRY** **LEATHER** **CAVE**
WINE TIPS	**PARING WITH DARK CHOCOLATE AND DRIED CHERRIES** e.g. Fino / Manzanilla sherry, Port, Sauternes, Chocolate Stout

MORE TASTE MAKERS

As we already said in the introduction, there aren't enough pages in this book to portray every cheesemaker and affineur. Below you'll find an alphabetical list, by country, of the producers who we have not been able to do justice to in this book but who certainly deserve to be mentioned. Followed by seven more taste profiles of cheeses which simply had to be incorporated in the book.

BELGIUM

Fromagerie du Gros Chêne in Méan - *www.groschene.be*
Fromagerie du Troufleur in Waimes - *www.troufleur.be*
Het Dischhof in Diksmuide - *www.dischhof.be*
Het Hinkelspel in Gent - *www.hethinkelspel.be*
Kaasmakerij Catharinadal in Hamont-Achel - *www.catharinadal.be*
Merx Kaas in Lotenhulle - *www.facebook.com/MerxKaas*

GERMANY

Kaesekuche - *www.kaesedepot.de*
Hofkaeserei Kraus - *www.hofkaeserei-kraus.de*

FRANCE

Beurre Bordier in Saint-Maur-des-Fossés - *www.lebeurrebordier.com*
Comté Marcel Petite in Granges-Narboz - *www.comte-petite.com*
Comté Juraflore in Poligny - *www.juraflore.com*
Epoisses fermier GAEC des Maronniers in Origny
Ferme du port Aubry in Cosne-Cours-sur-Loire - *www.ferme-portaubry.fr*
Fromagerie Réo in Lessay - *www.réo.fr*
Les frères Marchand in Nancy - *fromages-freres-marchand.fr*
Le Vieux Berger in Roquefort-sur-Soulzon - *www.le-vieux-berger.com*
Pont L'Eveque en Pave D'Auge in Livarot-Pays-d'Auge - *www.fermedelamoissonniere.fr*

GREAT BRITAIN

Baron Bigod in Bungay - *www.fenfarmdairy.co.uk/cheese/*
Berkswell Cheese in Berkswell - *www.berkswell-cheese.myshopify.com*
Corra Linn in South Lanarkshire - *www.erringtoncheese.com*
Ducketts Caerphilly in Caerphilly - *www.westcombedairy.com/cheddar*
Gorwydd Caerphilly in North Somerset - *www.trethowanbrothers.com*
Isle of Mull Cheese in Tobermory - *www.isleofmullcheese.co.uk*
Keens Cheddar in Wincanton - *www.keenscheddar.co.uk*
Lincolnshire Poacher in Alford - *www.lincolnshirepoachercheese.com*
Montgomery's Cheddar in North Cadbury - *www.montgomeryscheese.co.uk*
Mrs Kirkham's Lancashire in Preston - *www.mrskirkhamscheese.co.uk*
Pitchfork Cheddar in Weston Super Mare - *www.trethowanbrothers.com*
Sparkenhoe Blue in Market Bosworth - *www.leicestershirecheese.co.uk*
Sparkenhoe Red Leicester in Hinckley - *www.leicestershirecheese.co.uk*
St James Cheese in Cartmel - *www.stjamescheese.co.uk*
Stonebeck Wensleydale in Nidderdale - *www.stonebeckcheese.co.uk*
Westcombe Cheddar in Evercreech - *www.westcombedairy.com/cheddar*
Whin Yeats Wensleydale in Carnforth - *www.whinyeatsdairy.com/home*

IRELAND

Cashel Farmhouse Cheesemakers in Fethard - *www.cashelblue.com*
Durrus Cheese in Bantry - *www.durruscheese.com*
Sheridans Cheese Mongers in diverse steden - *www.sheridanscheesemongers.com*

ITALY

Azienda Agricola Di Venti Pietro in Calascibetta: *geen website*
Azienda Agricola Petit Jacques Donato in Bionaz: *geen website*
Azienda Agricola Pontevecchio in Vidor - *www.pontevecchio.tv.it/negozio*
Azienda Agricola Stagnoli Francesco in Bagolino - *geen website*
Azienda Agricola Stutz & Pfister in Mombaldone - *www.robiolabio.com*
Azienda Gran Sasso in Castel del Monte - *www.aziendagransasso.com*
Borgoluce in Susegana - *www.borgoluce.it/prodotti/mozzarella-e-latticini-di-bufala*
Casa Madaio in Eboli - *www.casamadaio.it*
Gorgonzola Tosi in Gattico-Veruno - *www.caseificiotosi.it*
Eggemoa in Selva dei Molini - *www.eggemoa.com*
La Casearia Carpenedo in Camalò di Povegliano - *www.lacasearia.com*
La Meiro in Castelmagno - *www.terredicastelmagno.com*

THE NETHERLANDS

Boeren Goudse oplegkaas in het Groene Hart - *www.boerengoudseoplegkaas.nl*
De Kruidenwei in Nooitgedacht - *www.dekruidenwei.nl*
L'Amuse in Amsterdam en IJsmuiden - *www.lamuse.nl*

PORTUGAL

Azeitão Cheese
Beira Baixa Cheese
Castelo Branco Cheese
Évora Cheese
Nisa Cheese
Rabaçal Cheese
Serpa Cheese
Serra da Estrela Cheese
Transmontano Cheese
Tradifoods in Agualva-Cacém - *www.pt.tradifoods.com/Tradifoods*

SPAIN

Airas Moniz in Chantada-Lugo - *www.airasmoniz.com*
La Antigua in Fuentesaúco - *www.queserialaantigua.com*
Rey Silo in Pravia - *www.reysilo.es*
Sierra la Solana in Herencia - *www.queseria1605.com*
Xavier Campo in Tresviso - *www.quesodetresviso.com*

UNITED STATES

Columbia Cheese in New York - *www.makertomonger.com*
Formaggio Kitchen in Boston - *www.formaggiokitchen.com*
Uplands Cheese in Dodgeville - *www.uplandscheese.com*
Rogue Creamery in Central Point - *www.roguecreamery.com*

SWITZERLAND

Fromagerie Fleurette in Rougemont - *www.tommefleurette.ch*
Fromagerie Margot in Yverdon-les-Bains - *www.margotfromages.ch*
Guentensperger in Bütschwil - *www.guentensperger-kaese.ch*
Jumi in Vechigen - *www.jumi.lu*
Willi Schmid in Lichtensteig - *www.willischmid.ch*

TASTE PROFILE

COMTÉ AOP
Le Haut-Doubs

French hard cheese made from cow's milk affinated by Marcel Petite

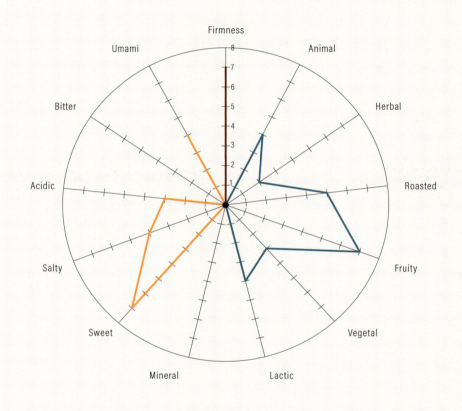

■ texture   ■ aroma   ■ flavour

TEXTURE	**FIRM AND SUPPLE**
DOMINANT FLAVOURS	**NUTS**
	CARAMEL
	ROASTED NUTS, BEURRE NOISETTE
	MEAT BROTH
SUBTLE NOTES	**CREAM, BOILED MILK**
	STRAW, HAY
	HEATHER
WINE TIPS	**OXIDATIVE WHITE WINE (*VIN JAUNE*)** e.g. type *Vin Jaune* (Savagnin)

TASTE PROFILE

MONT D'OR AOP
La Fruitière des Jarrons

A soft French winter cheese from cow's milk, bounded by a ring of pine wood. Also known as Vacherin du Haut-Doubs.

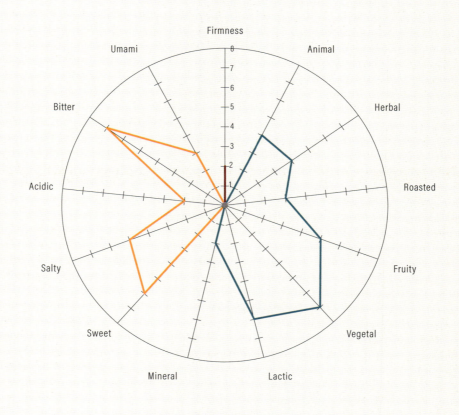

TEXTURE	**SOFT, RUNNY AND STICKY**
DOMINANT FLAVOURS	**PINE WOOD, RESIN**
	MUSHROOMS, WET HAY, HUMUS
	BEECHNUTS, WALNUTS
	FLOWERS
	COFFEE
	MILK, BUTTER
SUBTLE NOTES	**BARNYARD, LEATHER, WET WOOL**
	HERBS (CLOVE)
	FLINT
WINE TIPS	**FRESH RED WINE WITH SUPPLE TANNINS**
	e.g. Poulsard (Plousard), Trousseau, Zweigelts
	AGED RED WINE WITH TERTIARY AROMAS
	e.g. aged Nebbiolo, aged Sangiovese

TASTE PROFILE

ROQUEFORT LE VIEUX BERGER
Maison Combes

A French blue veined cheese made from sheep's milk

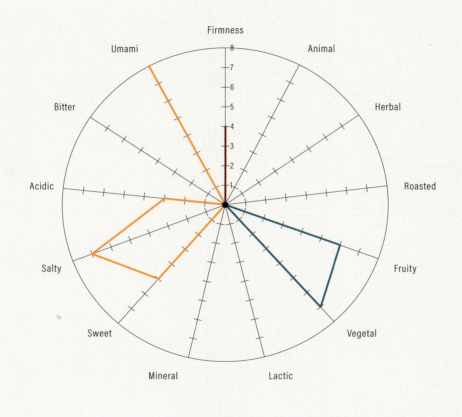

TEXTURE	**CREAMY AND GRAINED**
DOMINANT FLAVOURS	**WALNUTS, HAZELNUTS**
	MUSHROOMS, WET HAY, HUMUS
	BUTTER
SUBTLE NOTES	**ONION, LEEK**
WINE TIPS	**SWEET WHITE WINE WITH OR WITHOUT NOBLE ROT**
	e.g. type Sauternes or Passerillage (Reciot, Vin Santo, Vin de Paille)

TASTE PROFILE

LANGRES AOP
Fermier Remillet

A small, soft French cheese made from cow's milk from the Langres, in the Grand Est region

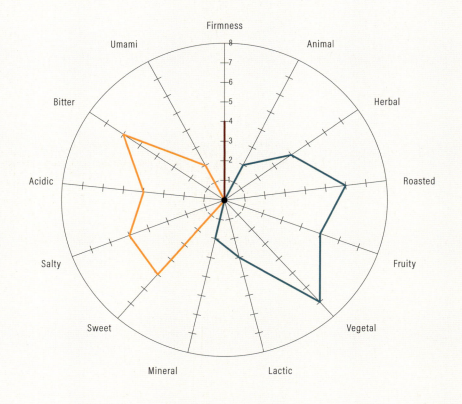

TEXTURE	**CLAYEY AND STICKY**
DOMINANT FLAVOURS	**GRASS, STRAW, WET HAY**
	NUTS
	FLOWERS
	COFFEE
	ROASTED ONION
SUBTLE NOTES	**BARNYARD, LEATHER, WET WOOL**
	BUTTER, CREAM
	EARTHY TONES
	HERBS
	WET STONES
WINE TIPS	**COMPLEX WHITE WINE WITH SPICY TONES**
	e.g. Gewürztraminer, Torrontés

TASTE PROFILE

ZAMORANO AOP
Quesería La Antigua

Hard Spanish sheep's cheese of the Manchego type made in Zamora in the region of Castilla and León

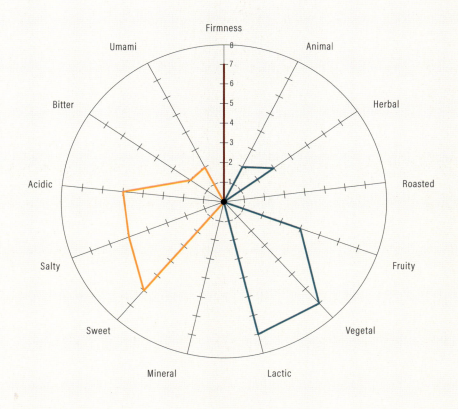

■ texture   ■ aroma   ■ flavour

TEXTURE	**FIRM AND GRAINED**
DOMINANT FLAVOURS	**GRASS, HAY** **YOGURT, MILK** **HEATHER** **NUTS**
SUBTLE NOTES	**BARNYARD** **WET WOOL**
WINE TIPS	**WHITE AROMATIC WINE WITH HIGH ACIDITY** e.g. dry Riesling or Sauvignon Blanc **SPICY RED WINE** e.g. GSM blend (Grenache, Syrah, Mourvèdre)

TASTE PROFILE

PICÓN BEJES-TRESVISO AOP
Javier Campo

A semi-soft, blue veined Spanish sheep's cheese from Tresviso in Cantabria

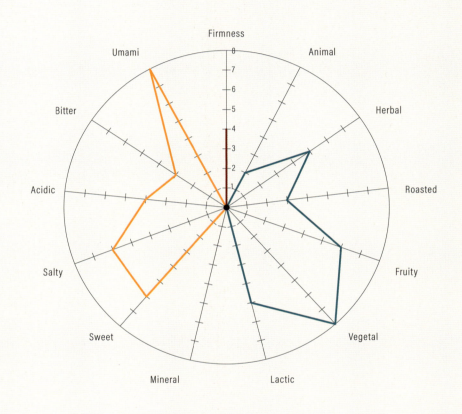

TEXTURE	**OILY AND GRAINED**
DOMINANT FLAVOURS	**WALNUTS, HAZELNUTS**
	MUSHROOMS, WET HAY
	BUTTER
	PEPPER, NUTMEG
SUBTLE NOTES	**BEURRE NOISETTE**
	MEAT BROTH
	STEWED ONION, STEWED LEEK
WINE TIPS	**FORTIFIED WINE**
	e.g. type Port or red Vins Doux Naturels

TASTE PROFILE

HUMO
Quesería Cultivo

Spanish sheep's cheese of the Cantal type

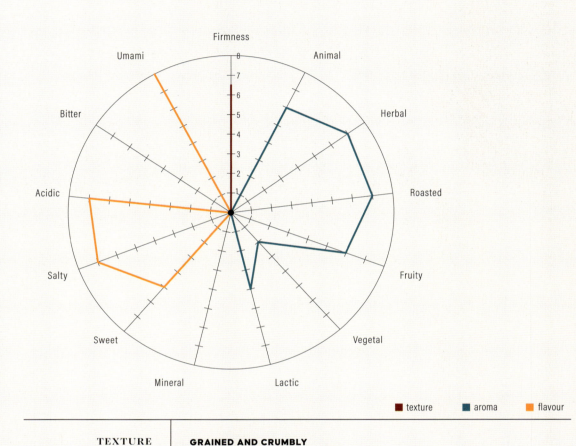

TEXTURE	**GRAINED AND CRUMBLY**
DOMINANT FLAVOURS	**STEWED MUSHROOMS** **MEAT BROTH / SMOKED MEAT** **HAZELNUT / ALMOND, WALNUT** **TOAST, BRIOCHE** **PEPPER** **PEANUT BUTTER**
SUBTLE NOTES	**PINEAPPLE** **BUTTER, BOILED MILK** **HAY, STRAW** **ONION** **EARTHY TONES**
WINE TIPS	**SWEET WHITE WINE WITH NOBLE ROT (*BOTRYTIS*)** e.g. type Sauternes (Sauvignon Blanc, Sémillon, Muscadelle) or Trockenbeerenauslese (Riesling) **SWEET WINE MADE OF DRIED GRAPES (PASSERILLAGE)** e.g. Vin de Paille, Vin Santo and Recioto

Acknowledgements

The road between dream and reality is often riddled with practical barriers. In our case, it was initially Brexit and later the COVID pandemic that were responsible for this book's four-year journey from inception to publishing. On the other hand, it allowed this project to mature just like real cheese. We hope this book will be enjoyed just as much as the unique cheeses it describes.

We would also like to take a moment here to thank the people whose careful and dedicated contributions led to this result.

To all the cheesemakers and affineurs who wanted to share their stories with us; artisans who, despite their busy lives, made time to take up their pens.
Johan Ghysels and *Yaele Vanhuyse* from Lannoo, for immediately and enthusiastically jumping on the bandwagon from the first moment we contacted them with this idea for a book.
Jason Hinds from *Neal's Yard Dairy*, who wrote the foreword and travelled from London to Antwerp in February 2019 to provide moral support for our idea.
Charlotte Nauwelaerts, for her expertise in developing the taste profiles.
Photographer *Kris Vlegels* and designer *Grietje Uytenhouwen*, for turning this book into a beautiful whole.
Lotte De Snijder, for the coordination and for initially editing all the submissions for this book, without whom this book would never have been published.

As the initiators of this project, we also want to personally thank several people who have played a role or have been a significant source of inspiration on our cheese journey.

Giedo De Snijder

Many thanks go out to *Fried* and *Freya* and their team at *Elsen Kaasambacht* in Leuven, Belgium. They have supported me in so many ways over the last thirty years.

Jean-Charles Arnaud, CEO of *Comté Juraflore* and the standard-bearer of French cheese culture. A man with noblesse who exudes grandeur with every fibre of his being and inspired me no end with what he had to say about the essence of the cheesemaking and maturation process, such as *essayer de comprendre* and *le travail du detail*.

Frédéric Van Tricht:

First of all, I want to thank my parents, *Michel* and *Jeannine*, for inoculating me with cheese culture. My mother always took care of the customers in the shop so that my father could travel to visit cheesemakers and affineurs. My father laid the foundation that I continue to build on today. A big thank you for supporting me in everything I do and providing me with advice and help every step of the way.

My wife, *Veerle*, who has been my right hand in our business for several years and manages to combine that work with raising our son, Ruben.

Our team, which works hard every day to make Van Tricht the fine business it is today, particularly Peter and Karl, who have been a part of our team for over 20 years.

WWW.LANNOO.COM

Register on our website and we will regularly send you a newsletter with information about our latest books as well as interesting, exclusive offers.

Text coordination: Giedo De Snijder, Lotte De Snijder and Frédéric Van Tricht
Taste profiles: Charlotte Naulaerts
Translation: Textcase, The Netherlands
Photography: Papil – Kris Vlegels (cover, images taste profiles and pages 8, 10, 12, 16, 32, 222, 224, 228, 246)
Graphic design: Papil – Grietje Uytdenhouwen

Images cheese producers (with exception of taste profiles):
Karditsel (Maarten Deckers), Kaasaffineurs Van Tricht, Remeker, Almnäs (Jesper Anhede), Cravero, Formaggi Debbene, L'Etivaz, Neal's Yard Dairy (Harry Darby), Stichelton Dairy, Holden Farm Dairy (Harry Darby), Appleby's Dairy, Fromagerie Dongé, Joseph Paccard, Mons Fromager & Affineur, Jasper Hill Farm

If you have any comments or questions, please contact our editors:
redactielifestyle@lannoo.com
© Uitgeverij Lannoo nv, Tielt, 2022
D/2021/45/473 - NUR 440
ISBN: 9789401479578

All rights reserved. Nothing from this edition may be reproduced, recorded in an automated database and/or published in any form or in any way, whether electronic, mechanical or in any other manner without the prior written permission of the publisher.